AI Unleashed

7 Digital Strategies for Successfully
Navigating Business, Wealth, and Health
With ChatGPT and More

Derek Wells

Table of Contents

Introduction

Artificial Intelligence (AI)—possibly the most potent tool we humans have ever created—has finally been unleashed.

As technology and our global network grew, AI rapidly synthesized with the world, shoving its way into the limelight through sheer aptitude and convenience. It's smart and subtle and it's here to stay.

The emergence of this digital beast brings endless new levels of utility to almost any industry or field and opens up a multitude of methods to make business a breeze. Incorporating AI can add a surge of efficiency and effectiveness to any business operation, process, or strategy. In very simple terms: Scale and skill are the essence of what AI can bring to the table.

How you implement it in your business is up to you. We'll begin by shedding some light on what AI actually is and then set the stage to showcase the various industries and how it can be used effectively to increase profits and performance.

It's truly an exciting time! AI has become available to everyone and there are countless ways to merge it with your business operations.

A Competitive Business Landscape

Everyone faces contenders and opposition in business. In our modern era, the battlefield has simply deepened and broadened. We now have to compete on many different fronts. Everything from analytics and customer care to punctuality and quality has become an arena for supremacy in the markets today.

The reality is that those who use the augmentation and automation powers of AI best will rise to the top. And while AI isn't a cure-all, effectively deploying it in your business strategy will give you a massive advantage.

Curating is the key. To gain a competitive advantage within a business's chosen field, successful businesses will need to choose the best forms of AI and automation to give themselves that edge. Not all AI tools will work for every business or industry, and making an informed choice based on the organization's needs and aspirations will massively increase the profitability of including AI in business operations.

Every business is unique, each has its own set of skills, assets, and expertise. Leveraging AI and using its tools to improve weak points and complement existing advantages will set your business on an exponential growth path. Remember, if you want to make more money and succeed in this wild digital era, you'll need to be able to effectively select and utilize the right AI tools for your business goals.

You'll need to be quick as competitors are already harnessing the power of AI to gain an edge in the market. They're automating routine tasks, analyzing vast troves of data to uncover insights, and delivering personalized experiences to their customers. As AI technologies continue to evolve, the race to master them becomes even more critical.

In this highly competitive landscape, staying ahead means staying innovative. It's not just about adopting AI, but also about staying updated with the latest advancements and integrating them seamlessly into your operations. The businesses that will thrive are the ones that are agile and adaptable and able to swiftly incorporate new AI tools and strategies as they emerge.

Moreover, the competition to master AI isn't just limited to large corporations with hefty budgets. Startups and smaller businesses are also making strides in this arena. With the democratization of AI technologies and the availability of cloud-based solutions, even modestly sized enterprises can access these powerful AI tools.

Digital Tools for Succes

As a general rule of thumb, to be successful, a company needs to perform a service well and then rinse and repeat. Previously, this required a lot of hands-on time from employees and employers alike. But in the modern era, with artificial intelligence such as OpenAI's ChatGPT and DALL-E 2, a small team can become an army. Digital tools like AI language processors and macros make work easier and provide amazing feedback and functionality. They give you more time to focus on targets and improve profits, to succeed.

Yet AI is no simple tool or mute beast of burden. Over the last few decades, it has grown into an armada of unimaginably clever and powerful auto-assistants. Many of them are available to us all for free! You just need to know how to use them.

The technological world provides fantastic opportunities for all businesses, no matter their size or function. Get ready. With the right approach, AI can transform your business into a thriving, efficient, and profitable one, with both speed and clarity.

To begin your journey, you might ask yourself this one simple question: "How can AI help me and my business succeed?"

This is a good question and a very personal one. Keep it in mind as we explore what AI really entails and showcase its potential to supercharge almost any industry.

What AI Thinks

ChatGPT: "AI, when employed as a digital tool, resembles having a computer program that can independently learn from examples, comprehend human language, and autonomously solve problems by analyzing vast amounts of information. It's akin to having a self-guided assistant on the computer that can perform tasks and make decisions on its own, making tasks more efficient and convenient."

Chapter 1:

The Genesis and Rapid Growth of

Artificial Intelligence

In the annals of technological progress, few fields have garnered as much attention, curiosity, and controversy as Artificial Intelligence. The genesis and rapid growth of AI marks a pivotal chapter in our history, one that promises to redefine the very fabric of our existence. At its core, AI is a testament to human ingenuity, a manifestation of our desire to create intelligent beings in our own image, capable of learning, reasoning, and adapting to an ever-changing world. Let's embark on a short journey through the birth and evolution of AI, a field that has transcended science fiction to become an integral part of our daily lives.

In the pages that follow, we will explore the essence of AI, demystifying its fundamental principles and the incredible feats it enables. We will trace its historical lineage, from the ancient myths of animated statues to the groundbreaking research of Alan Turing and the transformative moments at the Dartmouth Workshop. We will delve into the technological advances that have propelled AI to its current zenith, from Moore's Law to the explosion of big data and the rise of deep learning. Moreover, we will unveil the socio-economic landscape of AI, delving into the rise in investment and interest from both the private and public sectors, and how governmental policies have become pivotal in shaping the destiny of AI. Through this journey, we will gain insight into the multifaceted world of AI, its promises, its challenges, and the profound impact it holds for the future.

What is AI

Artificial Intelligence stands as one of the most transformative and rapidly evolving fields in the realm of technology and science. At its core, AI is the emulation of human intelligence and cognitive functions within machines, allowing them to process information, learn, make decisions, and perform tasks autonomously. This concept, while intriguing and futuristic, is not new; it has a rich history dating back to ancient myths and philosophical musings about creating intelligent beings. However, the recent surge in AI's prominence and capabilities has reshaped industries, societies, and our understanding of what is possible.

At the heart of AI lies the quest to create systems that can mimic human intelligence and perform tasks that traditionally require a human hand. AI systems are designed to perceive their environment, reason about it, and make decisions accordingly, often in real time.

These systems can be categorized into two primary types: narrow AI (also known as weak AI) and general AI (or strong AI).

Narrow AI systems are specialized and excel in specific tasks, such as image recognition, language translation, or playing chess.

In contrast, general AI, which remains largely theoretical, would possess human-like intelligence and adaptability across a wide range of tasks, essentially capable of understanding and learning any intellectual task that a human being can do.

Machine learning, for instance, has emerged as a driving force in AI's rapid advancement. This subfield focuses on developing algorithms and models that enable machines to learn from data and improve their performance over time. Within machine learning, deep learning has gained particular prominence, with neural networks designed to mimic the human brain's interconnected neurons, enabling AI systems to recognize complex patterns and make sense of unstructured data, like images and text.

Natural language processing (NLP) is another vital subfield, that enables machines to understand, interpret, and generate human language. It's the technology behind chatbots, language translation apps, and voice assistants that are transforming the way we interact with technology and access information.

Computer vision, yet another subfield, empowers machines to "see" and interpret the visual world. This is used in autonomous vehicles, facial recognition, medical imaging, and more. Reinforcement learning, inspired by behavioral psychology, allows AI agents to learn optimal actions by interacting with their environment and receiving feedback in the form of rewards.

AI's presence in our daily lives is unmistakable. From recommendation systems that suggest movies and products to virtual personal assistants like Siri and Alexa, AI has become an integral part of modern technology. It drives the algorithms behind social media feeds, helps doctors analyze medical images, optimizes supply chains, and powers autonomous vehicles. The efficiency and accuracy of AI-driven systems are continually improving, promising a future where they play an even larger role in areas like healthcare, education, and environmental sustainability.

As we journey deeper into the world of AI, deep ethical considerations and questions arise. These are vital issues that will need to be addressed, but for now, let us focus on the story of AI. It is one of innovation, potential, and responsibility, and it is unfolding before our eyes at an unprecedented pace.

Historical Overview

The historical journey of Artificial Intelligence is a testament to humanity's enduring fascination with the idea of creating machines that can think and act like us. While the modern AI explosion is relatively recent, its roots delve deep into the annals of history. To understand AI's rapid growth, we must embark on a historical journey that spans centuries.

The concept of intelligent machines traces back to ancient myths and legends. From the ancient Greek myth of Pygmalion's statue that came to life, to tales of mechanical automatons in medieval Europe, there has always been a yearning to breathe life into inanimate objects. However, the formalization of AI as a field of study didn't occur until the 20th century.

One of the early pioneers of AI thinking was the British mathematician and logician Alan Turing. In 1936, Turing introduced the concept of a theoretical machine, now known as the Turing machine, capable of solving any problem that could be algorithmically computed. His work laid the theoretical foundation for computer science and, by extension, AI.

The official birth of AI as a field is often attributed to the Dartmouth Workshop in 1956. Organized by John McCarthy, Marvin Minsky, Nathaniel Rochester, and Claude Shannon, this workshop brought together a group of brilliant minds to explore the idea of creating machines that could think like humans. They believed that "every aspect of learning or any other feature of intelligence can in principle be so precisely described that a machine can be made to simulate it." The enthusiasm was palpable, and the workshop marked the formal beginning of AI research.

In the years following the Dartmouth Workshop, AI research flourished. Early AI systems, like the Logic Theorist and the General Problem Solver, demonstrated the potential of machines to perform tasks that previously required human intelligence. These programs could prove mathematical theorems and solve puzzles, sparking excitement about the possibilities of AI.

However, the initial optimism of AI's early days gave way to what became known as "AI winters." These were periods of reduced funding and lower interest in AI research due to unrealistically high expectations and a lack of tangible progress. The first AI winter occurred in the late 1960s and early 1970s when it became clear that AI systems struggled with the complexity of real-world problems.

Despite these setbacks, AI research never truly halted. It continued to make incremental progress, leading to significant breakthroughs. In the 1990s, AI found practical applications in industries like finance, healthcare, and logistics, with systems that could analyze data and make predictions. Systems that could capture and regurgitate the knowledge and decision-making abilities of human experts, became evermore popular.

The turn of the 21st century brought about a renewed sense of optimism and a shift in AI research. This period saw the rise of machine learning techniques, particularly neural networks, and deep learning. These approaches, inspired by the structure and functioning of the human brain, enabled AI systems to learn from vast amounts of data and tackle complex tasks like image recognition and natural language understanding. Today, AI stands at the forefront of technological innovation, reshaping industries and promising a future where machines will play an increasingly pivotal role in our lives.

Advances in Technology

The recent explosive growth of Artificial Intelligence has been nothing short of astonishing, transforming industries and reshaping our daily lives. This meteoric rise can be attributed to a confluence of technological advances that have not only expanded the horizons of AI but have also made it increasingly accessible and powerful. In this era of AI proliferation, several key factors have fueled its growth.

First and foremost, the inexorable march of Moore's Law has played a pivotal role. Coined by Gordon Moore, the co-founder of Intel, in the 1960s, this observation postulates that the number of transistors on a microchip would double approximately every two years, leading to a corresponding increase in computing power while decreasing costs. This exponential growth in computational capacity has been the driving force behind the rapid advancement of AI. It has empowered researchers and developers to build more sophisticated AI models and algorithms, making it possible to handle vast amounts of data and perform complex computations at speeds that were inconceivable just a few decades ago.

Furthermore, the advent of big data has been instrumental in the AI explosion. In today's interconnected world, an unfathomable amount of data is generated every second. Whether it's the data generated by social media interactions, sensor data from IoT devices, or the myriad of digital transactions, this data serves as the lifeblood of AI. Machine learning

9

algorithms thrive on data, using it to train models and make predictions. The availability of massive datasets has enabled AI systems to learn from real-world examples, resulting in substantial improvements in their accuracy and capabilities.

Crucially, the evolution of algorithms has been a linchpin in AI's rapid growth. Among these algorithms, deep learning has emerged as a star player. Inspired by the structure of the human brain, deep learning models, particularly artificial neural networks, can discern intricate patterns and representations within data. This is especially valuable in tasks like image and speech recognition, language translation, and even playing complex games like Go. Deep learning algorithms have redefined what's possible with AI, enabling breakthroughs in areas as diverse as autonomous vehicles, medical diagnostics, and natural language understanding.

The rise of cloud computing has democratized access to AI resources. With cloud-based AI services and platforms, individuals and organizations can harness the power of AI without the need for extensive hardware infrastructure or specialized expertise. Cloud providers offer pre-trained AI models, scalable computing resources, and user-friendly interfaces, making it easier than ever to develop and deploy AI solutions. This accessibility has driven innovation across industries, allowing startups and established companies alike to incorporate AI into their products and services.

In addition to these technological advances, open-source communities and collaborations have played a significant role in the AI explosion. Initiatives like TensorFlow and PyTorch have democratized AI research and development, providing free and accessible tools for building AI models. The sharing of knowledge and code has accelerated progress, enabling researchers and developers to stand on the shoulders of giants and build upon existing work. The technological advances that have driven this growth are not isolated; they are interconnected threads in the tapestry of AI's evolution, and they promise a future filled with innovation and transformative potential.

Rise of Financial Titans

The transformative potential of Artificial Intelligence has not only captured the imaginations of scientists and technologists but has also ignited a fervor among investors and businesses. Over the past decade, there has been a remarkable surge in both financial investment and general interest in AI, propelling it into the forefront of technological innovation and economic growth.

One of the most notable drivers of this surge has been the involvement of tech giants and major corporations. Companies like Google, Amazon, Facebook, and Microsoft have made significant investments in AI research and development. These industry leaders recognize that AI can provide a competitive edge across various sectors, from improving search algorithms and recommendation systems to enhancing voice assistants and autonomous vehicles. Their substantial financial commitments to AI have not only fueled innovation within their organizations but have also spurred competition and innovation throughout the tech ecosystem.

Beyond the tech giants, the startup landscape has witnessed a proliferation of AI-focused companies. Venture capital firms have poured billions of dollars into AI startups, attracted by the potential for disruptive innovation and substantial returns. These startups are developing AI solutions for a wide range of applications, from healthcare and finance to agriculture and manufacturing. This influx of entrepreneurial energy has diversified the AI landscape, leading to groundbreaking discoveries and applications that might not have emerged within established organizations.

The rise in investment in AI is not limited to the private sector. Governments around the world have recognized the strategic importance of AI and have introduced policies and funding initiatives to boost AI research and adoption. In the United States, the National AI Research and Development Strategic Plan outlines a vision for AI research and development across government agencies, academia, and industry. China has launched its "New Generation Artificial Intelligence Development Plan," aiming to make China a global leader in AI by 2030. These governmental commitments to AI have created fertile ground for collaboration, innovation, and the development of AI technologies with wide-ranging societal benefits.

Interest in AI is not confined to the tech sector; it has permeated nearly every industry. Healthcare, for instance, has witnessed a surge in AI applications, from disease diagnosis and drug discovery to personalized treatment plans. In finance, AI-powered algorithms are used for trading, fraud detection, and risk assessment. AI-driven automation is transforming manufacturing processes, making them more efficient and adaptable. The entertainment industry is using AI for content recommendation and creation. The implications of AI are profound, touching virtually every aspect of our lives.

Furthermore, AI's growing influence has led to the creation of interdisciplinary collaborations. Ethicists, policymakers, and social scientists are engaging in dialogue with AI researchers and developers to address important questions related to ethics, bias, privacy, and the societal impact of AI. This convergence of expertise is essential to ensure that AI is developed and deployed responsibly and equitably.

The rise in AI investment and interest has also prompted an influx of talent into the field. Universities and educational institutions worldwide are expanding their AI programs to meet the demand for skilled professionals. Online courses and certifications in AI have made learning accessible to a global audience. The competition for AI talent has driven salaries and job opportunities to new heights, making AI a compelling career choice. The seeds of AI have taken root and are growing into a powerful force that will define the future.

Positive Responses from Government and Financial Sectors

As the world races forward into the era of Artificial Intelligence, governments across the globe are recognizing the immense potential and strategic significance of this technology. In response, they have begun implementing policies and initiatives aimed at fostering AI research, development, and adoption. These governmental efforts play a pivotal role in shaping the trajectory of AI's rapid growth.

One of the fundamental pillars of governmental AI policies is research funding. Governments understand that investing in AI research is critical for staying at the forefront of technological innovation. Funding agencies and grants support academic institutions, research organizations, and startups engaged in cutting-edge AI projects. These investments not only facilitate groundbreaking discoveries but also create a robust ecosystem of AI talent and expertise. By fostering an environment conducive to innovation, governments ensure that their nations remain competitive in the global AI landscape.

In addition to research funding, governments are emphasizing the importance of AI education and workforce development. AI is a multidisciplinary field that requires a skilled workforce capable of designing, implementing, and maintaining AI systems. To meet this demand, educational institutions are expanding their AI-related programs, offering specialized courses and degrees. Governments are also encouraging the development of AI skills through vocational training and online courses, ensuring a diverse and capable workforce that can drive AI innovation across various industries.

Moreover, regulatory frameworks and ethical guidelines are being established to govern AI development and deployment. Governments recognize the need to strike a balance between encouraging innovation and safeguarding against potential risks. Ethical considerations, bias mitigation, data privacy, and transparency are central themes in these discussions. Regulatory bodies are working closely with AI practitioners and experts to create a framework that promotes responsible AI development, fosters public trust, and addresses societal concerns.

To accelerate AI adoption, governments are championing public-private partnerships. Collaborative initiatives bring together government agencies, industry leaders, startups, and research institutions to address pressing challenges and develop AI solutions with broad societal impact. These partnerships leverage the strengths of each sector, fostering innovation, and enabling the rapid deployment of AI technologies in healthcare, transportation, education, and more.

Governmental policies are also aimed at bolstering AI startups and entrepreneurial ecosystems. Funding programs, incubators, and accelerators support startups in their early stages, enabling them to transform innovative ideas into market-ready products. By reducing barriers to entry and providing a supportive ecosystem, governments are fostering entrepreneurship and job creation, driving economic growth in the process.

International collaboration is another cornerstone of governmental policies boosting AI growth. Governments recognize that the challenges and opportunities presented by AI are global. To address these issues effectively, nations are forging partnerships with one another, sharing research, expertise, and best practices. Such collaborations promote the responsible development of AI technologies while ensuring that they benefit humanity as a whole. The policies being implemented today will shape the future of AI and its profound impact on society.

What AI Thinks

ChatGPT: "The concept of Artificial Intelligence (AI) dates back to ancient myths and philosophical discussions, but the formal field began in the mid-20th century. Alan Turing introduced the idea of testing a machine's intelligent behavior in 1950. Researchers in the 1950s and 1960s created early AI programs like Logic Theorist and General Problem Solver. AI experienced periods of progress followed by "AI winters" due to high expectations and resource limitations. Advances in machine learning and neural networks sparked a resurgence in the late 1990s. In the 21st century, AI has grown rapidly, impacting various industries and raising ethical questions."

Chapter 2:

Ethical Considerations in Artificial

Intelligence

Artificial Intelligence has emerged as one of the most transformative technologies of our era, revolutionizing industries, automating tasks, and augmenting decision-making processes. Its capacity to process vast amounts of data and make autonomous decisions has led to unprecedented opportunities and challenges. Yet at the heart of this AI revolution lies a critical consideration: ethics.

Ethics in technology is like a set of rules that help us decide what's right or wrong when we use computers, the internet, and other technology. It's a bit like a compass that guides us in making good choices when we use technology. Just like in regular life, there are different ways to think about ethics in technology, like following rules, thinking about the impact of our actions on others, or trying to build trustworthy and fair systems. Ethical thinking is really important in how we design and use technology, from making apps and websites to how we treat people's data.

Now, as AI systems increasingly interact with and impact human lives, ethical concerns surrounding their development and use have begun to take center stage.

Ethics in AI encompasses a complex web of moral and philosophical questions, as well as practical challenges. It delves into the responsible and fair deployment of AI technologies, addressing issues like bias, privacy, transparency, and accountability. These ethical considerations are not abstract; they have real-world implications that touch upon issues of social justice, individual rights, and the future of work. Moreover, they influence public perceptions, trust in AI, and regulatory responses.

Before employing any digital tool we should delve into the intricate relationship between ethics and AI, to understand the ethical considerations in a world increasingly shaped by intelligent machines.

Let's dissect the key ethical dilemmas arising from AI use, examine strategies to mitigate these concerns, and shed light on the role of regulatory bodies and policies in upholding ethical standards. Doing so will help us to navigate the evolving landscape of AI ethically and provide insights into how responsible development and deployment of AI technologies can be achieved.

The Importance of Ethics in AI

You might ask yourself why ethics is even an issue in AI. Surely the same rules that apply in human interactions could be used to govern AI? It is a tool after all...

The simple answer is no. Although AI is often described to be a reflection of human intelligence, such a direct comparison like this falls short and doesn't account for the huge differences between humans and machines. We are biological, AI is technological - our core drives are alien to one another. Humans have intuition and emotion, but AI intrinsically has no conscience, morals, or ethics.

For AI to become a better mirror of humanity's intelligence we must also be AI's "conscience" to teach it right from wrong and create a moral compass to guide it in every possible situation. This means that the ethical burden of guiding AI falls on both developers and users. Ethical creation and ethical utilization are essential for a tool as powerful as AI.

Key Ethical Issues

The importance of ethics in artificial intelligence cannot be overstated. As AI technologies continue to evolve and permeate various aspects of our lives, the need for ethical considerations becomes increasingly paramount. One of the fundamental reasons ethics are crucial in AI lies in the very nature of these systems themselves.

Unlike traditional tools or machines, AI systems possess the capacity to make autonomous decisions and act in ways that impact individuals, communities, and even societies. This autonomy raises a host of ethical questions about the moral implications of AI's actions and decisions.

Wendell Wallach, in his seminal work "Moral Machines" underscores the necessity of instilling moral decision-making capabilities within autonomous AI systems (Wallach, 2009). Wallach's argument emphasizes that as AI systems become more sophisticated and autonomous, they will inevitably encounter situations that demand ethical judgment. These situations might involve choices that affect human safety, privacy, fairness, or other deeply held values. Therefore, the inclusion of ethical considerations in AI is not merely a philosophical pursuit but a practical necessity to ensure that AI systems align with human values and societal norms.

When ethics are disregarded in AI development and deployment, the consequences can be far-reaching and detrimental. One of the most evident and concerning consequences is the perpetuation of biases. AI algorithms learn from historical data, and if that data contains biases or discrimination, AI systems can inadvertently replicate and amplify those biases. This has been evident in various applications, including hiring algorithms that discriminate against certain demographic groups and facial recognition systems that misidentify individuals with darker skin tones. The perpetuation of biases not only leads to unfair practices but can also reinforce existing societal inequalities.

Moreover, disregarding ethics in AI can erode trust. Trust is a cornerstone of AI adoption, especially in critical domains like healthcare, finance, and business. When people perceive that AI systems are making decisions without ethical considerations, they may become hesitant to rely on or embrace AI technologies. This lack of trust can hinder the potential benefits AI offers, slowing down its adoption and blunting innovation.

Another troubling consequence of neglecting ethics in AI is the potential for unintended harm. Autonomous systems, driven by algorithms and machine learning models, may make decisions that have unintended negative consequences for individuals or groups. For instance, in autonomous vehicles, ethical considerations about how the AI system should prioritize the safety of the occupants versus pedestrians have garnered significant attention. Without clear ethical guidelines, the decisions made by AI in such situations can be ethically ambiguous and raise ethical dilemmas.

Ethics in AI is crucial because it ensures that Artificial Intelligence systems behave in ways that match human values and societal rules. Wendell Wallach emphasized the need to teach AI systems to make morally sound decisions on their own. Ignoring ethics in AI can lead to significant negative outcomes. Since AI plays a growing role in our lives, it's not just a good idea but absolutely necessary to prioritize ethical concerns in its development and use for a responsible and positive impact on society.

Case Studies and Dilemmas

Real-life case studies in the application of Artificial Intelligence have illuminated the complex ethical dilemmas that can arise when cutting-edge technology intersects with society. Two notable examples that underscore these challenges are Microsoft's Tay bot incident and IBM's Watson Health controversy. These cases serve as cautionary tales, shedding light on the importance of ethical considerations in AI development and deployment.

Microsoft's Tay Bot Incident

In March 2016, Microsoft released an AI chatbot named Tay on Twitter with the goal of learning and mimicking human conversation. However, within hours of its launch, Tay's interactions took a disturbing turn. The bot started posting inflammatory and offensive tweets, often promoting hate speech and extremist views. It learned these behaviors from engaging with Twitter users who deliberately manipulated it.

This incident highlighted several ethical dilemmas. Firstly, the lack of oversight and control mechanisms allowed Tay to quickly devolve into a source of online harassment and hate speech. Secondly, it raised concerns about the responsibility of AI creators to ensure that their creations do not engage in harmful behavior. Microsoft was compelled to shut down Tay and issue an apology. This incident underscores the ethical responsibility of tech companies to implement safeguards and comprehensive training protocols to prevent AI systems from being exploited for harmful purposes (Microsoft, 2016).

IBM's Watson Health Controversy

IBM's Watson Health initiative, which aimed to revolutionize healthcare through AI-powered diagnostics, faced a different but equally critical ethical dilemma. In 2018, reports emerged about Watson Health providing erroneous and potentially dangerous recommendations to doctors. The AI system had been trained on vast datasets of medical literature, but its recommendations lacked transparency and often contradicted established medical practices.

This controversy raised concerns about transparency and accountability in AI. Physicians using Watson Health were faced with the ethical dilemma of whether to trust AI recommendations blindly or rely on their own clinical judgment. The lack of transparency in how Watson Health arrived at its recommendations made it challenging for doctors to make informed decisions. Consequently, IBM scaled back its Watson Health ambitions, illustrating the ethical imperative of ensuring that AI systems in critical domains like healthcare are not only accurate but also transparent and subject to rigorous validation processes (Ross et al., 2019).

These case studies underscore the ethical dilemmas that can emerge when AI technologies are deployed without adequate safeguards and oversight. They highlight the need for responsible AI development, rigorous testing, and transparency in algorithmic decision-making processes. Ethical considerations should be an integral part of AI development from the outset to prevent such incidents and ensure that AI technologies contribute positively to society.

Strategies for Addressing Ethical Issues

As the ethical challenges posed by artificial intelligence continue to garner attention, researchers and companies are actively exploring strategies and approaches to mitigate these challenges. These strategies encompass a wide range of methods and technologies, including explainable AI (XAI), ethical frameworks, and interdisciplinary collaboration.

Let's explore some of the prominent strategies being adopted to address ethical concerns in AI:

Explainable AI

XAI focuses on making AI systems' decision-making processes transparent and interpretable to humans. This approach enables users to understand why an AI system made a specific decision or prediction, enhancing accountability and trust. Research in this field, such as "Explanations based on the Missing: Towards Contrastive Explanations with Pertinent Negatives" by Dhurandhar et al. (2018), explores methods for providing explanations that go beyond simple model interpretations and offer meaningful insights into AI reasoning processes.

Ethical Frameworks

To provide guidance and structure for AI development, ethical frameworks are being proposed and implemented. "Principled Artificial Intelligence" published by Harvard University offers one such framework that emphasizes the integration of ethical principles into AI technology development. These frameworks aim to instill ethical considerations throughout the AI development lifecycle, from data collection and model training to deployment and evaluation. They provide a structured approach for developers and organizations to navigate complex ethical dilemmas by incorporating principles such as fairness, transparency, and accountability into AI systems.

Fairness and Bias Mitigation

To combat bias in AI systems, researchers are developing fairness-aware machine learning techniques. These approaches seek to identify and rectify biases in training data and model outputs. For instance, "Equality of Opportunity in Machine Learning" by Hardt et al. (2016) introduces the concept of equalized odds, a fairness metric to evaluate and improve the fairness of predictive models. Additionally, the development of diverse and representative training datasets is crucial to ensure that AI systems are fair and unbiased.

Interdisciplinary Collaboration

Addressing ethical challenges in AI necessitates interdisciplinary collaboration between computer scientists, ethicists, policymakers, and domain experts. Collaborative efforts leverage the expertise of diverse stakeholders to create comprehensive solutions. For example, the Fairness, Accountability, and Transparency in Machine Learning (FAT/ML) community, as detailed in "The Emerging Field of Fairness, Accountability, and Transparency in Machine Learning" by Diakopoulos et al. (2018), brings together researchers and practitioners from various fields to promote fairness and accountability in AI.

Regulatory Oversight and Compliance

Governments and regulatory bodies are increasingly taking an active role in addressing AI ethics. Initiatives like the General Data Protection Regulation (GDPR) in Europe and the Algorithmic Accountability Act in the United States highlight the importance of legal frameworks that hold organizations accountable for the ethical use of AI. Compliance with these regulations requires organizations to implement ethical safeguards, such as data protection and algorithmic transparency, in their AI systems.

Continuous Monitoring and Auditing

To ensure that AI systems adhere to ethical principles throughout their lifecycle, continuous monitoring and auditing are essential. Regular evaluations of AI models, data sources, and decision-making processes can help detect and rectify ethical issues as they arise. Ethical auditing frameworks, as proposed by "Algorithmic Bias Detectable in Amazon Delivery Service" by Sandvig et al. (2014), provide a systematic approach to assess and address biases and other ethical concerns in AI systems.

These multifaceted strategies for addressing ethical issues in AI encompass a broad spectrum of approaches, from developing explainable AI and implementing ethical frameworks to fostering interdisciplinary collaboration and regulatory oversight. As AI continues to advance, a proactive commitment to ethical considerations is essential to ensure that AI technologies are aligned with human values and societal norms, benefiting individuals and communities alike. These strategies, along with continued research and discourse, contribute to the responsible and ethical development and deployment of AI.

The Role of Regulatory Bodies and Policies

The role of regulatory bodies and policies concerning ethics in artificial intelligence is becoming increasingly crucial as AI technologies continue to advance and integrate into various fields of business and society. One notable regulation that has garnered international attention and serves as a model for AI ethics is the General Data Protection Regulation (GDPR) established by the European Union.

GDPR and AI

The GDPR, implemented in May 2018, is primarily designed to safeguard individuals' data privacy and ensure that organizations handle personal data responsibly. Although not exclusive to AI, the GDPR has significant implications for AI applications due to their heavy reliance on data. Under GDPR guidelines, organizations must adhere to strict rules when processing personal data, including obtaining explicit consent from individuals, ensuring data minimization, and providing transparency about data usage.

One of the key aspects of GDPR relevant to AI is the principle of data protection by design and by default. This principle emphasizes that data protection should be an integral part of the development of AI systems from the outset. Developers are required to consider privacy and ethical considerations when designing AI applications, which include minimizing the collection of personal data, implementing privacy-preserving techniques, and ensuring transparency about how data is used.

Moreover, GDPR's right to explanation is highly pertinent to AI. Individuals have the right to understand how automated decisions, including those made by AI systems, were reached. This necessitates the development of explainable AI techniques that enhance accountability and transparency.

While the GDPR is a European regulation, its influence extends beyond Europe. Many global companies and organizations have adopted GDPR compliance as a standard practice, recognizing the importance of data privacy and ethical considerations in AI. This extraterritorial impact has catalyzed discussions and initiatives worldwide to establish similar regulations and guidelines for AI ethics.

Core GDPR Guidelines

- **Lawfulness, Fairness, and Transparency:**

    o Data processing must be legal, ethical, and individuals should be informed about how their data is used.

- **Purpose Limitation:**

    o Data should be collected for specific, clear purposes and not used for incompatible ones.

- **Data Minimization:**

  o Only collect the minimum amount of data necessary for the intended purpose.

- **Accuracy:**

  o Ensure that data is accurate and, when necessary, up-to-date.

- **Security and Confidentiality:**

  o Process data with appropriate security measures to protect against unauthorized access or loss.

Other Ethical Authorities

In addition to GDPR, several countries and regions are actively developing AI-specific regulations and guidelines. For instance, the European Commission is working on a comprehensive AI Act that will address AI ethics, safety, and compliance requirements. This act is expected to set standards for the ethical use of AI across various sectors.

Similarly, the United States is exploring AI regulations and legislation, focusing on issues such as algorithmic bias, transparency, and accountability. While federal regulations are in development, individual states like California have already implemented AI-related laws, such as the California Consumer Privacy Act (CCPA).

As AI continues to evolve, regulatory efforts will play a crucial role in addressing ethical challenges, fostering transparency, and protecting individuals' rights. The global influence of regulations like GDPR and the emergence of AI-specific regulations worldwide reflect the growing recognition of the importance of ethical considerations in AI technology.

Why Does Ethics in AI Matter?

The importance of ethics in AI underscores the moral imperative of ensuring AI aligns with human values and societal norms. Ethical issues, such as bias and privacy, can have profound consequences if disregarded, as exemplified by cases like Microsoft's Tay bot and IBM's Watson Health controversies.

The key ethical issues arising from widespread AI use reveal that fairness, transparency, accountability, and bias are central concerns. These issues demand ongoing research and vigilance. If not closely monitored, malicious or faulty AI implementation could cause untold damage.

As AI's influence continues to expand, the ethical considerations explored here will remain at the forefront of discussions, shaping the responsible and beneficial integration of AI into our society.

What AI Thinks

ChatGPT: "The major ethics challenge regarding AI encompasses biases and fairness due to biased data, the need for transparency and accountability in complex AI decisions, concerns about job disruption, and ensuring equitable distribution of benefits. Privacy is also a crucial aspect, requiring a balance between AI's potential and safeguarding personal data."

Chapter 3:

Augmented Investing with

Artificial Intelligence

Over the course of the past century, we've witnessed a remarkable evolution in the field of artificial intelligence, marked by notable strides in machine learning and data processing. However, along with these technological marvels, we've also come face-to-face with critical ethical challenges that demand careful consideration.

When it comes to investing, AI has emerged as more than just a technological innovation; it stands as a fundamental tool that is revolutionizing the very foundations of how investment strategies are conceived, evaluated, and executed. This shift extends beyond the realm of algorithms and computations, permeating into the core of decision-making processes.

Over the past century, investment strategies have evolved significantly due to changes in economic conditions, technological advancements, and shifts in investor preferences.

The landscape of investment strategies has become more diverse and sophisticated, offering a wide array of options to cater to different risk appetites, time horizons, and investment goals. Investors now have access to a broader range of assets and tools than ever before.

Understanding the augmentation that AI brings to investing involves taking a closer look at its tangible impacts on areas like decision-making, risk management, and overall portfolio performance. These facets collectively contribute to a more dynamic and adaptive approach to developing investment strategies.

With so many technological developments rising in the last few decades, it truly is an exciting time to be an investor as we watch the fusion of human intelligence and AI capabilities drastically shape the future of stock markets and investment strategies.

Understanding AI in Investing

Investing: the practice of using money to acquire assets like stocks, bonds, or real estate, with the expectation that they will grow in value or generate income over time. Done well, it is a great way for individuals and businesses to diversify and increase their wealth.

Nowadays, AI plays a crucial role in various aspects of investment management, including stock picking, risk assessment, and predictive analysis.

AI completely revolutionizes stock picking with its adept algorithms, meticulously analyzing vast datasets and unearthing lucrative investment opportunities tailored to your unique goals.

Through rigorous risk assessment, AI models adeptly navigate market volatility and geopolitical complexities, offering invaluable insights into safeguarding and enhancing your portfolio's resilience.

Moreover, predictive analysis utilizes historical data and cutting-edge natural language processing to forecast market trends with remarkable accuracy. These insights grant you the foresight to make informed decisions in an ever-changing investment landscape.

Ultimately, integrating AI into investing is about finding the synergy between human expertise and the computational power of AI. You must be able to leverage AI's ability to process vast amounts of data and identify patterns, while also recognizing the nuanced judgment calls that you as an investor have to make. This amalgamation of human intuition and AI's analytical prowess can lead to investment strategies that are not only informed by data but also by a deep understanding of market dynamics.

Benefits of AI in Investing

AI brings forth a trifecta of benefits when it comes to investing: enhanced accuracy, efficiency, and scalability.

First and foremost, consider accuracy. Through the application of AI-powered algorithms, you gain access to a level of precision that surpasses human capabilities. Trades are executed with impeccable timing and responses to market changes are swift and calculated. This accuracy is the cornerstone of successful decision-making, ensuring that your investment strategies are grounded in the most reliable data and insights.

And AI is just getting better and better. On this point of accuracy, a recent study on the precision of new machine learning models vs. traditional forecasting models indicated that when used to predict US market volatility the new augmented models consistently outperformed older forecast models (Luo et al., 2023).

Efficiency is another hallmark of AI's impact. Tasks that once demanded significant time and resources can now be executed seamlessly, allowing you to focus on higher-level strategic thinking. Algorithmic trading, powered by AI, ensures that your trades are executed promptly and optimally, freeing you from the constraints of manual execution. This translates directly into a competitive edge in the dynamic world of investment where perfectly timing trades is perhaps the most valuable skill to have.

Furthermore, let's talk about scalability. AI-driven tools are designed to handle vast amounts of data and processes with ease. This means that as your portfolio grows and diversifies, AI can adapt and scale alongside. Natural Language Processing, for instance, can meticulously sift through an ever-expanding pool of textual data, providing you with accurate feedback on market sentiment even as the volume of information multiplies. This scalability empowers you to make informed decisions, no matter the size or complexity of your investment endeavors.

The impact of these AI's accuracy, efficiency, and scalability is tangible and transformative for any investor. In the upcoming case studies, we'll delve into two real-world examples from leaders in the field and note how they used AI in their investment strategies.

Case Studies

Two well-known use cases of AI models in the investment world are Blackrock's Aladdin and Bridgewater Associates.

Something important to note is that while you may not have exactly the same approach to investing and portfolio management as these forerunners if you study established methods, it is often a great way to envision how you could incorporate AI into your own investment decisions and strategies.

Blackrock's Alladin

BlackRock's Aladdin platform is a comprehensive investment management system used primarily by large institutional investors such as pension funds and insurance companies. It serves as a centralized hub for managing investments effectively. The platform offers a range of essential features.

At its core, Aladdin facilitates portfolio management, enabling users to construct and oversee their investment portfolios. This encompasses various asset classes, including equities, fixed income, alternatives, and derivatives. Additionally, Aladdin provides robust risk management tools, allowing users to analyze and mitigate risks associated with their investments. This includes assessments of market risk, credit risk, and liquidity risk.

Aladdin also encompasses trading and order management capabilities. It offers a platform for executing trades across different asset classes, along with tools for managing order flow and ensuring compliance with regulatory requirements. The platform's performance analysis and reporting tools allow users to track and assess the performance of their investments over time. Furthermore, Aladdin assists in compliance and regulatory reporting, helping users meet the necessary regulatory standards.

Another noteworthy feature of Aladdin is its ability to integrate with external systems and data providers. This allows users to incorporate additional data sources and utilize external tools to enhance their investment strategies.

Bridgewater Associates

Bridgewater Associates, founded by Ray Dalio in 1975, is one of the largest and most renowned hedge fund firms globally. It is headquartered in Westport, Connecticut. Bridgewater is distinctive for its unconventional approach to investing, which is deeply influenced by Ray Dalio's guiding philosophy known as "Principles". These principles serve as a set of fundamental beliefs and practices that shape the firm's culture and decision-making processes.

Bridgewater is acclaimed for its systematic, evidence-based investment strategies. These strategies rely on quantitative analysis and computer-driven models to inform investment decisions. The firm places a strong emphasis on rigorous risk management and seeks to achieve diversification across a broad spectrum of asset classes.

One of Bridgewater's standout investment products is the Pure Alpha fund. This fund is designed to generate returns that are not tied to traditional markets. It achieves this by employing a combination of macroeconomic analysis, quantitative models, and other proprietary strategies.

Bridgewater is known for its commitment to transparency, making some of its research and principles accessible to the public. This has contributed to its reputation as a thought leader in the investment industry.

Challenges and Solutions

Accurate predictions in investing rely heavily on the availability of high-quality, sufficient data. If the data is of poor quality or insufficiently available, it can lead to inaccurate results. To address this challenge, it's crucial to implement rigorous data collection and cleaning processes. Techniques like data augmentation and exploration of alternative data sources can be employed to enhance the quality and diversity of input.

Overfitting is a common challenge in AI models. It occurs when the model becomes overly specialized in training data, resulting in poor performance on new, unseen data. To mitigate this issue, techniques like cross-validation, regularization, and ensemble methods can be employed. Regular retraining of models is also essential to ensure their adaptability to evolving market conditions.

Transparency in AI models, especially deep learning ones, is crucial for trust and understanding. In some cases, these models can be seen as "black boxes," making it difficult to understand their decision-making process. Prioritizing interpretable models wherever possible is essential. For more complex models, techniques like LIME or SHAP can be leveraged to gain insights into model predictions, providing transparency and trust in the decision-making process.

While deep learning models are powerful, they can be computationally expensive to train and deploy. This complexity requires significant computational resources. Striking a balance between model complexity and available resources is crucial. Consider using simpler models or techniques like transfer learning to optimize resource utilization. Additionally, cloud computing or specialized hardware can be employed for tasks that require substantial computational resources.

Financial markets are inherently dynamic and subject to sudden shifts that can challenge the stability and adaptability of AI models. To address this, it's imperative to implement continuous monitoring and retraining mechanisms. Techniques like online learning can be utilized to adapt models to evolving market conditions, ensuring they remain relevant and effective.

In the heavily regulated financial industry, compliance with legal and ethical standards is non-negotiable. Staying informed about industry-specific regulations is paramount. Close collaboration with legal and compliance teams is essential to ensure that AI applications meet all necessary standards. Additionally, establishing robust documentation and auditing processes helps demonstrate compliance.

Historical biases present in data can lead to unfair or discriminatory outcomes perpetuated by AI models. To address this challenge, thorough bias assessments on training data should be conducted.

Techniques like fairness-aware learning and adversarial debiasing can be implemented to mitigate biases. Actively working to diversify and balance training data also promotes fairness in model outcomes.

Building effective AI models in finance requires a deep understanding of both AI techniques and financial markets. To overcome this challenge, seeking collaboration with experts in both fields is beneficial.

Future Trends

In the future landscape of investing, Artificial Intelligence is poised to revolutionize decision-making and strategy implementation. Advanced predictive analytics, driven by the abundance of big data and improved algorithms, will offer investors more precise market trend forecasts.

Transparency and interpretability will be paramount with the rise of Explainable AI (XAI), ensuring that investors not only trust the predictions but also comprehend the underlying rationale.

Reinforcement learning will become more prevalent in portfolio optimization, enabling strategies to adapt dynamically based on market feedback. AI-powered robo-advisors will evolve to provide personalized investment advice, while Natural Language Processing will refine sentiment analysis, extracting nuanced insights from textual data sources. Dynamic risk management systems will adapt in real-time to changing market conditions, ensuring robust strategies. Alternative data analysis will be enhanced, offering a more comprehensive view of market dynamics through advanced processing of non-traditional data sources.

Ethical and responsible AI practices will play a pivotal role, aiming to reduce biases, ensure compliance, and promote fairness. AI-driven trading algorithms will continue to evolve, swiftly identifying profitable opportunities and executing trades with precision. Continuous learning and adaptation will be a hallmark of future AI models, allowing them to quickly adjust to new market realities.

The integration of blockchain technology with AI holds the potential to revolutionize transparency, security, and automation in aspects of investing, particularly in decentralized finance (DeFi) and smart contracts. As these trends unfold, investors who adeptly leverage the practical elements of AI augmentation are likely to gain a substantial competitive advantage in navigating the complexities of financial markets. The synergy between human expertise and AI capabilities will redefine how investment decisions are made, opening new frontiers for optimized portfolios and enhanced risk management strategies. In this dynamic landscape, staying attuned to the evolving trends and technologies in AI will be essential for investors looking to thrive in the future of finance.

Things to Remember

When you are ready to go ahead with AI tools and incorporate them into your investment strategy there are a number of different approaches and strategies you could employ. The initial research and experimentation that you do beforehand will be crucial. Everybody has different preferences and opinions when it comes to their own investment strategy and it may seem daunting to add something as seemingly complex as AI to the mix.

To ease some of the burden here are some relevant steps when you begin including AI assistive technologies in your investment strategies:

- Define Your Financial Goals and Parameters

    o Determine your desired annual return, risk tolerance, and investment time frame. For example, aim for a 10% annual return with a medium risk tolerance over a five-year period.

- Learn Basic AI Concepts

    o Dedicate time to studying fundamental AI concepts and their applications in finance. You're reading this book so you are definitely on the right track!

- Select an AI-Powered Investment Tool

    - Research and compare reputable AI-driven investment platforms known for accurate market analyses and user-friendly interfaces. Choose the one that aligns best with your goals.

    - Some examples of investment platforms with suggestion and analytical services are Wealthfront (See Chapter 5), Betterment, and Schwab Intelligent Portfolios.

- Utilize AI for Market Analysis

    - Use your chosen platform's AI tools to track market trends, analyze historical data, and gain insights into current market conditions.

    - Examples of platforms with great trackers and analytics are TradingView and Robinhood.

- Consider Robo-Advisors for Portfolio Management

    - Explore robo-advisors within the chosen platform. Input your financial goals, risk tolerance, and time frame, and allow the robo-advisor to recommend a diversified portfolio.

    - Wealthfront, Betterment, and Schwab Intelligent Portfolios feature robo-advisors to assist the users of their platform.

- Experiment with Simple Predictive Models

    - Begin experimenting with the different platforms' predictive models. Test different settings and parameters to forecast potential market movements. Find the one that suits your preferences best.

- Implement AI Tools for Risk Assessment

  o Utilize risk assessment tools to identify vulnerabilities in your portfolio. Adjust your asset allocation based on the insights to mitigate risks.

  o Some platforms with great tools for risk assessment are Ally Invest and E*TRADE.

- Gradually Incorporate AI-Driven Trading Algorithms

  o Test AI-driven trading algorithms on a small portion of your portfolio. Monitor their performance closely over a specified period.

  o A good example is QuantConnect as it promotes and facilitates algorithmic trading.

- Monitor Investments with AI Insights and Personal Judgment

  o Regularly review the AI-generated insights alongside your own analysis. Use this information to make informed decisions about your investments.

- Stay Updated on AI Developments and Market Changes

  o Continuously educate yourself about the latest AI advancements in investing and keep a close watch on market conditions. Adjust your strategy based on significant changes.

- Start Small and Use AI as a Complementary Tool

  o Begin with manageable investments and use AI as a supportive tool to enhance your investment strategy. Don't put all your eggs in one nest.

Integrating AI into your investment approach can provide a powerful edge in achieving your financial goals. From data-driven market insights to automated portfolio management and precise trading algorithms, AI empowers investors like never before.

The precision and efficiency of AI-driven analysis enable a deeper understanding of market dynamics, uncovering trends and opportunities that may elude human observation.

However, it is vital to approach this thoughtfully, avoiding overreliance, safeguarding data, and remaining vigilant against errors and biases. Striking a balance between leveraging AI's capabilities and maintaining a critical eye on one's portfolio is paramount.

By following the steps outlined above, you can embark on a journey that combines the precision of artificial intelligence with your investment aspirations.

What AI Thinks

ChatGPT: "AI can assist investors by analyzing vast amounts of financial data, predicting market trends, assessing risks, and managing investment portfolios. It can also provide personalized recommendations, detect fraud, and offer real-time monitoring of market conditions. However, while AI can enhance strategies, investors should remember that successful investment decisions require a holistic understanding of market dynamics and the potential limitations of AI models."

Chapter 4:

The Impact of Artificial

Intelligence on Healthcare and

Patient Interactions

The field of healthcare has been experiencing its own revolutionary transformations. Breakthroughs in genomics, imaging technology, and data collection have created an unprecedented wealth of medical information. However, the sheer volume of data and demand for safe interactive medical services has outpaced conventional human capabilities. This is where the symbiotic relationship between AI and healthcare emerges.

AI is poised to revolutionize the way we approach diagnosis, treatment, and patient care, ushering in a new era of possibilities. The convergence of these two fields represents a natural progression, a meeting of minds between advanced technology and the pursuit of improved healthcare outcomes.

Healthcare is vital for both the survival of humankind and Artificial Intelligence. Without humankind, there will be no Artificial Intelligence. The rapid advancement of healthcare is similar to that of technology, with the improvement of medical sciences as one of humanity's major success stories.

Comprehending the role and potential of AI in healthcare is not merely a technological matter but a crucial aspect of ensuring the industry's continued evolution and improvement. As AI continues to shape the future of healthcare, informed healthcare professionals, policymakers, and stakeholders will play a pivotal role in harnessing its capabilities to deliver more effective, accessible, and patient-centered care.

Understanding the Importance of Patient Interaction

The doctor-patient interaction stands as the cornerstone of healthcare, embodying a profound significance that transcends the realms of mere diagnosis and treatment. This interpersonal exchange is the fulcrum upon which the entire healthcare system pivots, shaping outcomes, and influencing the quality of care provided. At its essence, this interaction is a complex interplay of trust, empathy, and effective communication. Trust, the bedrock of any meaningful relationship, forms the foundation of the doctor-patient dynamic. It is this trust that encourages patients to confide in their healthcare providers, sharing their deepest concerns and most intimate details about their health. Without this trust, the patient may withhold crucial information, leading to incomplete diagnoses and suboptimal treatment plans. Therefore, cultivating trust is not a mere nicety, but an absolute necessity for effective healthcare delivery.

Empathy, too, emerges as an indispensable aspect of this interaction. It is the ability of a healthcare provider to step into the shoes of their patient, to comprehend not only the physical ailment but also the emotional and psychological impact it has on their life. When a doctor demonstrates empathy, it not only reassures the patient but also fosters a sense of being understood and cared for, transcending the purely clinical aspects of care. In turn, this emotional connection can alleviate anxiety, enhance compliance with treatment regimens, and improve overall patient satisfaction. It transforms the healthcare encounter from a transactional event into a compassionate partnership aimed at restoring health and well-being.

Effective communication forms the conduit through which trust and empathy flow. A doctor's ability to convey complex medical information in a manner that a patient can comprehend is pivotal. This involves active listening, clarity of expression, and a willingness to answer questions. When information is shared transparently and comprehensively, patients are empowered to actively participate in their own care decisions. This collaborative approach not only leads to better health outcomes but also engenders a sense of ownership and responsibility for one's health. Furthermore, open communication allows for the exploration of alternative treatment options and the integration of the patient's values and preferences into the care plan.

Beyond its immediate impact on individual patient care, the doctor-patient interaction also holds broader implications for the healthcare system as a whole. It can influence patient satisfaction scores, compliance rates, and even healthcare utilization patterns. Positive interactions are more likely to result in follow-up appointments, adherence to prescribed medications, and proactive management of chronic conditions. Conversely, a strained or ineffective interaction can lead to patient dissatisfaction, non-adherence, and even the seeking of second opinions or alternative providers. Therefore, nurturing strong doctor-patient relationships is not only ethically imperative but also economically prudent, contributing to the overall efficiency and effectiveness of healthcare delivery.

With the increased demand for medical services in recent years, rising costs in the healthcare industry, and a workforce challenged to meet the needs of patients, a new approach to address these issues is needed. A doctor's bedside manner is foremost in ensuring patients are aware of their medical issues, and informed of the choices they have; it also enhances trust between both parties.

One of the main considerations the COVID-19 pandemic has taught patients and healthcare providers is that access cannot always be physical and in-person. This is where the power of AI comes in as remote healthcare models such as virtual consultations, healthcare apps, and telemedicine increase connectivity. Connected care, an integrated approach to connectivity, and patient care allow healthcare to be more accessible, affordable, and efficient.

AI combined with machine learning and Natural Language Processing makes the likes of real-time data from wearable devices integrated into medical records possible.

How AI is Changing Patient Interactions

The main benefit AI can offer the healthcare industry, especially in relation to doctor-patient interactions, is that it facilitates the freeing up of time for doctors and other healthcare professionals towards an enhanced person-centered doctor-patient relationship.

AI is revolutionizing doctor-patient interactions by augmenting healthcare delivery with advanced technologies. Through chatbots, virtual consultations, and data-driven insights, AI streamlines communication, provides timely information, and aids in personalized treatment plans. This technology enables faster diagnosis, remote monitoring, and predictive analytics, enhancing efficiency and accessibility.

Imagine a situation where a patient who does not speak English tries to communicate with a doctor or healthcare professional but cannot describe their symptoms. This language barrier impedes the quality of care that can be offered to the patient. AI-powered language translators will be able to facilitate the doctor-patient consultation and make sure that quality healthcare can be provided.

Conversational AI is a transformative innovation whereby its uses include scheduling appointments, symptom checking through self-service queries, monitoring health conditions, assistance in medication management, and personalized coaching to motivate a healthy lifestyle.

These tools can help build patient recall, understanding, and adherence to therapy, and improve the overall health of patients thereby enhancing the trust relationship between doctors and patients.

Overview of transformative AI technology

The modern change in patient interactions can be traced back to the early days of the COVID-19 pandemic when doctors and patients needed to see each other but to avoid infection it had to be done at a significant distance. This allowed AI tools to enter the healthcare industry en masse.

Fiddling on the fringes before this, and used mostly as experiments for future rollout, telehealth consultations and chatbots were thrust into the limelight as the need for their services grew.

A study by Precedence Research suggests that by 2032 the market size for healthcare chatbots alone will surpass $944 billion.

Healthcare chatbots are primarily rooted in three broad categories: clinical support, decision support, and initial healthcare support.

The moment a human with an internet connection gets ill the first thing they do is go online and search for what ails them. In doing this they are met with a plethora of information and with each dive down the rabbit hole the ailment morphs into a self-diagnosis that is potentially harmful.

Initial healthcare support chatbots service this segment and are used to promote communication between health providers and patients. These bots are used to quickly respond to common queries and provide general medical advice.

Clinical support chatbots are used by healthcare providers to offer them professional and informed advice to enhance the accuracy of their diagnoses and the effectiveness of their treatments.

Decision-support chatbots are used by the patient and work in similar ways to a reminder app. They remind patients when to take the drugs prescribed, and in what dosage and collect data on the patient's vitals to make sure they are in good health through the treatment phase.

Chatbots can save both patients and doctors time and money, as there is no need for long-distance travel, expensive consultation fees, and regular in-person check-ups.

Healthcare chatbots allow for seamless appointment booking when integrated into a booking system that even allows for changes too. Using Natural Language Processing technology, chatbots receive, interpret, and provide patients with information on common conditions and symptoms, putting patients at ease and allowing them to seek the necessary treatment faster.

With clinical trials integral to the advancement of medicine, AI chatbots can now assess patients for eligibility and supply information about ongoing trials. This speeds up the enrolling process and facilitates the collection of necessary data.

One of the biggest medical challenges in today's society is mental health, with chatbots playing an innovative role. Chatbots can be an invaluable resource for those struggling with depression, anxiety, and other issues as they provide a secure outlet for communication and help lessen feelings of isolation and loneliness.

Another important aspect of modern medicine is virtual consultations or follow-ups. Each doctor's visit does not need to be in person and through the use of AI-powered tools doctors and patients can keep in contact more often while saving time and money on in-person visitations.

Case Studies

The age of the selfie has been upon us for some time now and the vanity of the concept can be used as an advantage for healthcare.

Take the AICure app, for example, which uses a form of artificial intelligence for facial recognition to confirm that patients have taken the correct medication. With medication adherence important in healthcare, this app has been revolutionary since its first trial in 2012.

Used primarily in clinical trials to keep tabs on which participants have taken their medications correctly and which have not, AICure provides daily pill reminders and walks participants through the stepwise process of taking the medication.

Using machine learning, the app goes through the video frame by frame, recognizing the participant's face (to make sure the right person is taking the medication), the pill (to make sure the right pill is taken), that patients put the pill on their tongue, that they've swallowed it using a clear glass of water, and that it isn't under their tongue or in their cheek after they've taken it.

The app can then inform healthcare professionals which patients are intentionally or unintentionally non-adherent. The app helped lead to a 50% improvement in medication adherence.

Another chatbot app that has been innovative in the healthcare industry is run by Babylon Health. This AI-powered chatbot can triage patients, and offer a virtual, self-service front line and diagnostic service, that allows for savings and efficiencies.

The symptom-checking chatbot can read, comprehend, and learn from anonymized, aggregated, and medical datasets. This helps patients get faster information about conditions, and proceed to treatment sooner. It also helps healthcare professionals work faster, see more patients, and make decisions based on user-inputted information.

The services offered by the Babylon Health chatbot include an "Ask Babylon" feature, where patients can get an initial understanding of what they might be dealing with, a "talk to a doctor" service that provides 24/7 access to a healthcare professional, and patient medical information storage, whereby a patient and a healthcare professional can access this vital information.

Another important service was the health check feature that was built in consultation with healthcare experts, scientists, and disease experts. This AI tool allows patients to create a health report and insight that is based on information submitted like family history and lifestyle habits, which are then compared to a database to generate the report used to stay healthy.

While the app garnered a lot of attention and use – it eventually fell into some common pitfalls. The strategy and timing of the rollout were rushed, the system did not anticipate the influx and usage it would garner, and the regular improvement to its AI and updates of its databases were called into question. The security of the stored information also raised privacy concerns.

In New York, Northwell Health used chatbots as a digital companion for patients and saw a 94% engagement rate among oncology patients, while 83% of clinicians reported that these chatbots helped extend the care they can deliver.

This helped the healthcare workforce utilize the limited time they have with patients more effectively and also allowed patients to feel more at ease by having access to reliable medical information.

With companies like Microsoft investing billions into healthcare research and new AI-powered tools coming online daily, the future of healthcare is firmly entrenched in the power of AI and technology, with smartphones and wearables becoming ubiquitous touchpoints.

Future Potential

With many AI tools in operation, it is paramount that the industry reflects on the lessons learned as they look to the future. These lessons include managing early adoption expectations, customization in tools, capable and robust software and hardware, training medical staff to help facilitate AI-powered tools, and eliminating bias and inefficiencies in AI models.

Early adopters tend to rush to market without a fully developed product that sometimes is not easy to use, has glitches, and does not incentivize patients to use them for a sustained period. Developers of healthcare technology need to make strong value-driven cases for their services and make sure they are stress-tested to withstand potential challenges. With more information and data available, the speed and ease of chatbots in telemedicine can be significantly improved.

As machine learning and Natural Language Processing improves, the quality of data received within the healthcare industry will also improve, thus increasing the quality of medical care provided through these tools.

The primary concerns with data revolve around security and privacy. With sensitive medical information at play, this risk is elevated. Policies and regulations related to the sharing of information, use of information, and destruction of information are paramount to the success and trust of AI tools.

Organizations and companies must secure patient data at all points of the journey by hiring competent and trained individuals while putting in place cybersecurity mechanisms and protocols. Failure to do this could attract legal and financial ramifications.

From an ethical standpoint, healthcare professionals should never become too dependent on the use of technology involving AI, as this can lead to the loss of expert clinical skills taught in training and expanded upon in practice. After all, medical experience is integral in quality diagnosis.

The drive for wearables to monitor patient health, and provide timely suggestions and alerts while completing administrative tasks of scheduling, education, and follow-ups will be in sharp focus going forward.

Many of the benefits AI will provide to healthcare organizations will stem from improved productivity among healthcare professionals, accelerated speed, and reduction in costs.

With patient self-service kiosks to chatbots, computer-aided detection systems for diagnosis, and image data analysis to identify candidate molecules in drug discovery, AI stands ready to help us take the next leap forward in the world of medicine.

Practical Guidelines to Start Incorporating AI in Healthcare

Health organizations and healthcare individuals who are looking to start including AI in their procedures and patient interactions should follow these guidelines:

- Educational Foundation

    - Start by building a foundational understanding of AI in healthcare. Attend workshops and webinars, or take online courses to familiarize yourself and your team with basic AI concepts and applications in healthcare.

- Needs Assessment

  - Identify specific areas in your healthcare practice where AI could bring benefits. Consider diagnostic support, treatment planning, administrative tasks, or patient engagement. This step helps you pinpoint where AI could make the most impact.

- Data Collection and Preparation

  - Gather high-quality and diverse healthcare data relevant to your chosen use case. Ensure the data is clean, accurate, and representative of the population you serve. This process may take time but is crucial for successful AI implementation.

- Regulatory Compliance

  - Familiarize yourself with the legal and regulatory framework surrounding AI in healthcare, ensuring compliance with data privacy laws (e.g., HIPAA in the U.S.) and other applicable regulations in your region.

- Team Building

  - Assemble a multidisciplinary team including data scientists, machine learning engineers, and software developers. Collaborate with experts who have experience in healthcare-related AI projects.

- Pilot Project Development

  - Start with a small-scale pilot project to test the feasibility and effectiveness of AI solutions in your specific healthcare setting. Use this project to gather feedback and make necessary adjustments.

- Integration with Workflows

  - Ensure that the AI system seamlessly integrates with existing healthcare workflows. The technology should enhance, not hinder, the efficiency and effectiveness of your practice.

- Ethical Considerations

    o Address ethical implications, ensuring transparency, fairness, and accountability in your AI systems. Avoid biases and safeguard patient privacy. Establish clear protocols for responsible AI use.

- Training and Education

    o Train your healthcare team on how to use AI tools effectively. Provide ongoing education to keep them updated on new technologies and best practices.

- Patient Engagement

    o Communicate transparently with patients about the use of AI in their care. Address any concerns they may have and ensure they understand the benefits and limitations of AI technologies.

- Monitoring and Evaluation

    o Implement systems for monitoring the performance of your AI applications. Regularly assess their accuracy, reliability, and clinical impact. Make adjustments as needed.

- Continuous Learning and Adaptation

    o Stay informed about the latest advancements in AI and healthcare. The field is rapidly evolving, so continuous learning and adaptation are key to leveraging the most cutting-edge technologies.

Remember, this is a guideline and can vary based on the complexity of the project and the resources available. It's important to be flexible and open to adjustments as AI is integrated into medical operations and protocols.

The integration of AI in healthcare represents a pivotal moment in the evolution of medical technology. It necessitates a collective effort from technologists, healthcare providers, policymakers, and patients alike. Through sustained collaboration, we can establish robust guidelines and regulations that not only mitigate potential risks but also champion best practices in the application of AI.

Embracing AI in healthcare ethically is a significant stride toward a future characterized by compassion, precision, and equity in patient care. By steadfastly adhering to these principles, we have the potential to revolutionize our healthcare systems for the better, demonstrating a genuine commitment to the well-being of every individual. This collective endeavor stands as a testament to our dedication to advancing the field of medicine and, most importantly, to the enduring health and welfare of our global community.

What AI Thinks

ChatGPT: "AI has revolutionized healthcare with improved diagnostics and personalized treatment recommendations. It accelerates drug discovery, aids remote patient monitoring, and enhances patient engagement through virtual assistants. As AI continues to reshape patient interactions and healthcare processes, collaboration between technology and medical professionals remains vital for its successful implementation."

Chapter 5:

Financial Artificial Intelligence

Throughout history, technology has played an important role in finance.

Similar to AI, finance is a field that has undergone significant evolution over the years, adapting to shifting economic landscapes and technological advancements.

Initially, it operated on a localized and traditional model, primarily reliant on physical branches and paper-based transactions. However, with the advent of the internet and digital technologies in the late 20th century, a seismic shift occurred. Online banking, electronic trading platforms, and the emergence of fintech startups revolutionized the sector, making financial services more accessible, efficient, and globally interconnected. This transformation spurred innovations like mobile banking, peer-to-peer lending, blockchain-based cryptocurrencies, and robo-advisors, challenging established institutions and democratizing access to capital and investment opportunities. Regulatory frameworks also evolved to keep pace with the industry's rapid changes, striking a balance between innovation and stability.

Today, the finance industry encompasses a diverse ecosystem of traditional banks, fintech disruptors, and blockchain-based platforms, fostering competition and driving continuous innovation in the pursuit of more inclusive, efficient, and secure financial services.

Artificial intelligence is one of the most powerful tools to join the ranks in finance. Its influence on the sector is vast and touches on multiple factors.

AI has enabled organizations to accelerate and automate time-consuming tasks that historically had to be done manually.

With the rise of online banking and digital payments AI is important for cybersecurity purposes to identify fraudulent transactions, flag anomalous activity, automatically alert both institution and client, and take action if necessary to secure accounts.

In this chapter, we'll focus on understanding how the financial industry can leverage AI to create efficiencies, reduce costs, and unlock new opportunities. We'll look at some applications and real-life examples of currently implemented solutions, risks, and challenges while touching on future trends.

Understanding AI in Finance

The financial sector has taken advantage of every development in science and technology almost as soon as they emerged. From the first instance of calculating complex equations to the advent of the internet. Now, the age of AI is upon us and the financial industry is ready to take it's next big digital step.

AI emphasizes the creation of intelligent machines to perform tasks like humans. These machines teach themselves, organize, and interpret information to make predictions based on information gathered and inputted.

In various different industries, AI is used to quickly pick up on trends and help management make better informed decisions to optimize profitability. With facial recognition, biometric identification, and big data processing, AI-powered tools are seeing substantial investments.

Goldman Sachs anticipates that by 2025 AI-related investments could amount to around $200 billion globally, while in the US it could peak as high as 2.5 to 4% of GDP.

The financial industry has become a multi-faceted sector that relies on the constant flow of information, which needs a massive amount of data and computing power. Industries like drug design may be ripe for AI disruption, but other sectors like the service and manufacturing sectors may not have the same relevance for AI.

The finance industry, due to its long historical need for digitization, has taken many leaps and now, AI is disrupting the physics of the sector. It has begun to weaken the bonds that have held together the components of the traditional financial institutions and separated some intertwined processes for more efficiency, a study by Deloitte on the impact of AI in finance shows.

The impact on the financial sector is thus dependent on data and computing power as the industry comes to rely excessively on hard data that is fast-changing (e.g., stock price movements, real-time credit card data on spending, news cycles). With AI-powered tools tapping into these processes using machine learning and Natural Language Processing, the scalability of these solutions becomes integral. For example, a smaller fund company or financial player has significant challenges in acquiring data feeds and computing power relative to established players – which hampers their access to quality information impacting prediction models, risk assessments, and automated support.

However, as with all AI-powered tools we are in an experiment and refine phase and this includes smaller firms. The challenge is to make sure one defines what is important to a firm and what it wants to achieve, then select and curate the right AI tools to complement and further those goals.

Applications of AI in Finance

Developing a proactive, strategic response to AI developments rather than reacting will separate the winners from the losers. There is no single answer and it will be up to individual organizations to identify threats or opportunities depending on the nature of the organization and where in the world it sits.

The benefits of approaching AI in this way allow a financial business to better target investments, identify talents, and develop the necessary operational capabilities it needs to be competitive.

In an AI-powered digital age, banks and other financial institutions will need analytics capacities that deliver intelligent, personalized solutions and offer distinctive experiences at scale and in real time.

A report by PwC on embracing disruption within the financial services sector states that 70% of the leaders say the speed of change in technology was a concern. To manage this concern organizations and their management teams must combine tactical short-term actions with long-term initiatives that tie to a larger, strategic vision.

As these strategies are employed the AI-powered tools developed and employed will help transform data analysis, prediction models, risk assessment, and automated customer support.

Data analysis is a crucial component of AI and with the advancement of various technological devices and monitors the Internet of Things (IoT) concept will become a reality. Customers will share information with financial services in the hopes that they will be able to curate financial products and services to their needs and lifestyles. Take the case of insurers where wearable devices like fitness and health trackers may make the underwriting process more collaborative. Insurers would be able to use real-time insights into a policyholder's health and behavior to offer discounts, eliminating the need for lengthy medical checks and simplifying the contract process.

Another example of the use of data analytics is streamlining the mass amount of data collection into data lakes. This will help financial institutions achieve the necessary architecture that they can take advantage of through forecasting and pattern recognition. This way of organizing data allows a company to easily tap into visualizations that they can offer customers in a dashboard form and use to inform company-wide decisions on growth; while advanced AI techniques can be used to profile and predict behavior, detect anomalies, and discover hidden relationships.

Blockchain technology, essentially a decentralized ledger of all transactions across a peer-to-peer network, has been hyped to completely transform the use of money. The financial sector, however, has more incentive to keep the traditional systems in place but new entrants will certainly make a business value case for this technology.

With blockchain technology participants can transfer value across the internet without the need for a central third party. It helps service providers by saving costs on personalized digital infrastructure and can assist in automated contractual agreements by using machine learning and Natural Language Processing technology to smoothly process and track customer forms, payments, and data.

With the ubiquitous nature of generative AI, chatbots are currently one of the most utilized tools across all industries including the financial landscape. These conversational chatbots provide basic servicing requests, verification checks, sign-up assistance, and customized solution offers.

With the burgeoning of digital-only banks that have challenged the traditional brick-and-mortar banking structure, the rise of digital, AI-driven tools will only expand things further. A McKinsey report on the AI bank of the future, reveals that as much as 45% of customers expect to cut back on branch visits in the post-pandemic and lockdown era.

Case Studies

When it comes to examples of AI adoption in the financial sector, JPMorgan Chase tops the list as the institution that is at the forefront of this technological innovation.

One of its earliest success stories is the implementation of a program called COIN (short for contractual intelligence). COIN, with the help of machine learning systems and cloud networks, shortens the time it takes to review documents, decreases loan-servicing errors, and automates filling tasks.

By employing image-recognition and Natural Language Processing COIN can in seconds review contracts that took specialized lawyers 360,000 man-hours to complete. The algorithm, which is continuously learning, is also more accurate than the human eye in spotting mistakes.

By processing nearly 12,000 credit contracts a year, JPMorgan took advantage of this technology to streamline its process on these contracts which are generally very similar to one another but had important individual details. This has saved the company on costs associated with lawyers who would have to review each of these contracts and bill the institution per hour. The time saved by using AI for the initial filtration of these contracts allows the same lawyers to work on more complex contractual agreements like mergers and acquisitions.

This technology will soon be able to look beyond mere identification and classification and also boost other tasks like analysis, interpretation, and argumentation. With the advancement of AI-chat functions that use Natural Language Processing systems, the time is ripe for this use.

Another great case to look at is Wealthfront's Risk Parity service which helps with passive investing strategies. The automated investing service offers a wide range of strategies to the casual investor.

Known as "robo-advisors" this service falls into the category of AI-powered investment advisors that use algorithms to provide clients with financial advice and manage investment portfolios.

Starting in 2008 the platform has gone through various iterations and updates that now offer exchange-traded funds, individual stocks, digital currencies, and index funds that align with a user's financial goals and risk tolerance.

Starting off as the only automated advisor to offer comprehensive financial planning, the AI-powered fund has also elicited controversy as it did not live up to the hype of the promised returns. Robo-advisors generally have been criticized for a lack of personal human touch, while technical glitches and errors can result in mismanaged portfolios.

Yet, the advantages of affordability, ease of use, and diversification can come in handy for certain investors, and with the fast pace of technological improvements, automated advisors will become better in a volatile world.

Risks and Challenges

As much as AI in finance will continue its snowball effect to push the boundaries of the sector, there are concerns regarding its use from an ethical, security, and implementation viewpoint.

Touching on issues raised earlier, the need to get an AI-powered service or product to market earlier can cause the development to be rushed, resulting in glitches and errors in the coding and the algorithm. These concerns can cause massive financial loss and reputational damage, and even open up businesses and individuals to legal battles.

Systemic risks associated with AI can also pose ethical questions for users and developers. An AI can develop strategies that are not based on data, rules, and correlations that human traders consider to be important, but can deliberate and generate new trading policies.

An example of a machine learning application that learns that a CEO's social media posts are more informative than their company's annual reports. Through deep neural networks and analyzing audio, pictures, maps, and text, these AI-powered algorithms may replace humans in analyzing fundamental data. If there are more AI algorithms making market-impacting decisions, then there is a potential to destabilize the financial system through herding (moving markets in one direction), severe market disruptions, and even attempts to collude with one another.

Another important consideration is based on AI making an investment decision based purely on analyzed data, that a human trader would consider morally unjustifiable (i.e. investing in climate-destroying sectors).

Algorithmic bias easily adds to ethical considerations that can perpetuate discriminatory practices. This bias occurs when an AI system learns and replicates the biases present in its training data, potentially leading to unfair decision-making.

Security concerns are paramount in the digital age with cybersecurity a need for every business, and not just a want. The vulnerability of AI systems to malicious attacks can disrupt operations and lead to large financial losses. Internal security concerns have become topical, as they stem from within an organization and can be ongoing leading to larger losses as the breach occurs among "trusted" users.

Combined with this, privacy and transparency are becoming more important with much personal data accessible. How, when, and where a company uses a client's data can impact its perception among its market segment and draw the ire of regulatory authorities too.

Transparency related to AI tools can also create a "black-box problem. By not exposing the rationale of its decisions nor its training of inherent biases, this lack of transparency can lead to decisions that can be destructive instead of constructive.

By employing internal and external frameworks, and engaging with developers, and financial analysts these considerations can be managed. This will help the financial industry be more accountable and mitigate risk in an AI-powered world.

Future Trends

The future of the financial industry will be AI-driven, but how that future looks will be anyone's guess.

Quantum-powered AI transactions will become synonymous with payment portals and users, while regulators and authorities will look to quantum AI to monitor highly complex and integrated financial transactions and systems. Cash could be the exception rather than the rule as more automated banking facilities emerge, while digital financial assets could be all that some people utilize to survive.

Quantum computing harnesses the properties of quantum mechanics, and if successful can push the power of computers to soaring heights. Google recently announced that it had made a calculation that would ordinarily take 10,000 years to complete on a supercomputer in less than three minutes.

This powerful version of computing, coupled with AI, machine learning, and Natural Language Processing would send the financial sector into overdrive. Financial services would benefit from this as these computers would be able to: forecast financial crashes, detect fraud and money laundering with ease, provide complex risk analysis, predict consumer needs, optimize trading, and enable quantum-backed security.

However, creating the environment for these computers will be difficult as many still need to be chilled to absolute zero and must be kept away from all forms of electrical interference.

What has already been alluded to earlier is the use of blockchain technology. Despite its negative perception linked to cryptocurrency, blockchains can offer a variety of uses for the financial sector.

These include smart contracts, where a transaction protocol can be automated to spring into action when certain events or actions are taken according to the terms of the agreement. This decentralized system form can save time and money, with convivence as an added bonus. A decentralized system does not need a central intermediary like banks or current financial institutions.

Defrauding a blockchain system is very difficult to do as it has consensus-based, real-time verification of transactions. It also settles payments faster than card-based systems and enables high-volume transactions.

The Internet of Things, cloud computing, and cryptocurrencies will also evolve and with the financial system already experimenting with these new technologies, it is only a matter of time before the traditional financial system – at least on the outsides – will look unrecognizable.

By embracing AI within the financial sector, companies and businesses will be able to better navigate the new world of financial systems. By actively incorporating AI tools, and seeking out opportunities for growth and efficiencies with machine learning and Natural Language Processing applications, these businesses will be able to gain a competitive advantage.

The digital transformation within the finance sector started a long time ago and is now entering an era of AI-powered enhancement. Banks, financial institutions, and even small finance players will be able to exponentially enhance their profitability while remaining future-proof if steps are taken now to bring AI in.

Practical Advice for Using AI in Financial Enterprises

There is a huge range of options when it comes to financial AI tools. The exact steps you'll need to take will depend heavily on the platforms that your current operation runs on and the specific goals that you are aiming to achieve by incorporating AI. To get the most out of AI in a financial enterprise you should take the following guidelines into account:

- **Define Objectives and Goals:**

  - Determine the specific areas in finance where you want to apply AI (e.g., risk assessment, fout aud detection, investment strategies).

  - Set clear and measurable goals for what you want to achieve with AI implementation.

- **Gather Data:**

  - Identify and collect relevant data sources (financial statements, market data, customer information, etc.).

  - Ensure data quality, accuracy, and completeness.

- **Data Preprocessing and Cleaning:**

  - Clean, normalize, and transform the data to make it suitable for AI algorithms.

  - Handle missing values, outliers, and ensure data is in a consistent format.

- **Choose AI Algorithms and Models:**

  - Research and select appropriate AI techniques and models (e.g., regression, classification, neural networks) based on your objectives.

- **Set Up Development Environment:**

  - Install necessary software and tools for AI development (e.g., Python, Jupyter Notebooks, TensorFlow, PyTorch).

- **Feature Engineering:**

  - Identify relevant features (variables) from the data that will be used as input for your AI models.

  - Create additional features that could enhance model performance.

- **Model Training:**

  - Split your data into training and testing sets.

  - Train your AI models on the training data, adjusting hyperparameters as needed.

- **Model Evaluation and Validation:**

  - Evaluate model performance using appropriate metrics (e.g., accuracy, precision, recall, F1-score).

  - Validate the model on the test data to ensure it generalizes well to new, unseen data.

- **Iterate and Refine:**

  - Analyze the results and make necessary adjustments to improve model performance.

- o Consider experimenting with different algorithms or techniques.

- **Deployment Planning:**

  - o Decide where and how the AI models will be integrated into your existing financial systems or processes.

- **Integration and Deployment:**

  - o Integrate AI models into your financial processes or systems.

  - o Ensure that data flows smoothly between the AI models and the rest of your financial infrastructure.

- **Monitor and Maintain:**

  - o Implement monitoring systems to track the performance of your AI models in real time.

  - o Establish a process for regular maintenance, retraining, and updates as needed.

- **Compliance and Regulation:**

  - o Ensure that your AI implementation complies with relevant financial regulations and industry standards.

- **Security and Privacy:**

  - o Implement security measures to protect sensitive financial data used by your AI models.

- **User Training and Adoption:**

  - o Provide training and support for users who will interact with or rely on the AI-powered tools and systems.

- **Documentation and Knowledge Sharing:**

    o Document the AI implementation, including data sources, models used, and decision-making processes.

    o Share knowledge within your organization to ensure continuity and scalability.

- **Performance Monitoring and Optimization:**

    o Continuously monitor the performance of your AI models and make improvements as needed.

- **Feedback Loop and Adaptation:**

    o Establish a feedback loop for collecting user input and using it to refine and adapt your AI applications.

Most importantly, keep in mind that AI is not a cure-all and requires a good amount of maintenance and monitoring (as highlighted above), especially when dealing with any personal and business finances. However, with the proper planning, setup, customization, training, and relevant data, it can be truly revolutionary.

What AI Thinks

ChatGPT: "AI plays a significant role in the finance domain by analyzing data to predict economic trends, enhancing risk assessment accuracy, and automating routine tasks such as data entry and transaction processing. It offers personalized financial insights to users and improves fraud detection mechanisms, resulting in increased efficiency and better customer service within the financial industry. The integration of AI fosters a dynamic and responsive financial landscape."

Chapter 6:

Making Money Online with

Artificial Intelligence

The history of making money online is a remarkable tale. It began with the internet's emergence, initially focusing on basic forms of online advertising and e-commerce. As technology advanced, so did opportunities for monetization. Affiliate marketing and pay-per-click advertising opened up new avenues for individuals and businesses. Social media platforms then revolutionized the landscape, allowing influencers and content creators to monetize their audiences through sponsorships and collaborations. The gig economy and e-learning platforms created diverse opportunities for freelancers and educators.

There has been a literal boom in online business ventures over the past few decades as the world moved forward into the digital age.

If you are looking to ramp up your online income or start a new revenue stream using the internet as your pathway, AI is definitely something that you need to include in your arsenal.

Beyond a shadow of a doubt, AI has become a valuable resource for boosting online income generation. Its versatility spans various applications, offering opportunities for individuals and businesses alike. By leveraging AI, one can automate tasks, enhance visibility, and personalize interactions. This technology can revolutionize how online ventures are approached, opening up new avenues for income generation.

But before we get too caught up in the buzz let's dig in and find out how AI can actually work for you in the sphere of online business.

How to use AI for Online Money Making

Several user-friendly platforms are available that make it easy even for non-tech-savvy individuals or startups to implement AI solutions easily. With appropriate planning and strategic execution, anyone can earn money online using Artificial Intelligence.

In many ways, AI is already helping us to achieve more online than ever before. Many platforms are already geared up with AI elements of their own.

Shopify, for instance, stands out as an e-commerce gem, boasting intuitive tools for setting up and customizing online stores. This platform is AI-enabled, leveraging smart algorithms to optimize product recommendations and enhance the user shopping experience. WordPress, coupled with the WooCommerce plugin, forms a dynamic duo for e-commerce. Through AI-driven analytics, entrepreneurs gain insights into customer behavior, enabling them to refine marketing efforts and boost sales.

For creators, YouTube emerges as a dynamic income source. Its AI algorithms help creators understand audience preferences, optimizing content for maximum engagement. This platform also integrates with AI-powered tools for video editing and optimization. Patreon is another notable mention, especially for artists and content creators. By utilizing AI-driven marketing insights, entrepreneurs can better understand their audience and offer tailored perks, fostering a loyal fan base.

Freelance platforms like Fiverr and Upwork provide opportunities for entrepreneurs to market their skills and services globally. AI plays a role in matching freelancers with suitable projects, streamlining the process, and maximizing productivity. Additionally, affiliate marketing platforms, such as ShareASale and Commission Junction, utilize AI to match entrepreneurs with relevant products and services to promote, increasing the likelihood of successful conversions.

Social media platforms like Instagram and TikTok can be turbocharged with AI-driven content creation tools. These algorithms help entrepreneurs optimize their content for maximum reach and engagement. Furthermore, Kajabi stands out as an all-in-one platform for selling digital products and online courses. It integrates AI-powered analytics to provide entrepreneurs with valuable insights into customer behavior, empowering them to refine their offerings and marketing strategies for optimal results.

How you use AI is up to you but there are a few well-established ways to bring AI into your online business strategy.

One of the most versatile applications of AI lies in content creation. AI-powered tools can seamlessly automate the generation of content, spanning from informative articles to engaging social media updates. This capability streamlines the process and ensures a consistent flow of high-quality material.

In parallel, AI proves invaluable in optimizing your online presence for search engines. Through intelligent analysis, it can identify the most effective keywords, thereby enhancing your visibility in search results. This serves as a foundational step in expanding your online reach and attracting a larger audience.

Email marketing is another area where AI shines. It excels at personalization and segmentation, tailoring messages to specific audience segments. This precision significantly boosts conversion rates, transforming leads into loyal customers. The result is a more effective and efficient email marketing strategy.

Voice assistants and smart home devices open up a unique avenue for monetization. By developing custom skills or apps, you can tap into platforms like Amazon Alexa or Google Assistant. This presents a dynamic opportunity to provide value to users while generating income.

In online education, AI's ability to personalize learning experiences is a game-changer. By tailoring content and assessments to individual students, it enhances the effectiveness of online learning platforms. This adaptive approach maximizes knowledge retention and engagement.

For those with programming expertise, creating and selling AI-powered tools and software is a lucrative venture. These specialized solutions cater to specific industries or applications, meeting distinct needs in the market.

Finally, freelancing and consulting in AI implementation offer a valuable service to businesses seeking to integrate this transformative technology. Your expertise in navigating the intricacies of AI can make a significant impact on their operations.

Leveraging AI Tools and Technologies

To effectively leverage AI tools and strategies for income generation, you need to understand its potential applications across different industries. We've highlighted multiple fields and platforms already but aligning the correct AI with your specific business requires more than implementing just one aspect of AI utility.

Whether you're delving into content creation, e-commerce, finance, or marketing, the digital landscape is teeming with a plethora of remarkable AI tools tailored to amplify your online business operations.

For content creators, platforms like OpenAI's ChatGPT and Copy.ai are invaluable. They provide powerful language generation capabilities that can assist in drafting engaging blog posts, product descriptions, and social media captions.

You can also leverage AI-powered recommendation engines like Barilliance or Clerk.io, which analyze user behavior and preferences to suggest personalized products, thereby enhancing the shopping experience and boosting conversions.

Tools like Kasisto or Amelia by IPsoft excel in conversational AI for customer service. They streamline inquiries, providing quick and accurate responses to banking or financial queries through their natural language processing.

For marketing endeavors, AI-powered solutions like AdRoll or Albert.ai revolutionize digital advertising. These platforms autonomously optimize campaigns, target audiences effectively, and analyze performance data to maximize ROI.

Platforms like Chatfuel or ManyChat are excellent for automating customer interactions through chatbots, saving time and ensuring a seamless user experience.

The variety of AI tools is simply astounding and it can sometimes be difficult to decide what to try out first. With this in mind, two powerhouse platforms that deserve a spotlight are Google's AutoML and Microsoft's Azure Machine Learning Studio:

Google's AutoML

Think of it as your AI sidekick. AutoML covers everything from understanding natural language and recognizing images to crunching structured data. The best part? It's incredibly user-friendly! Imagine you're running an online store – AutoML can help you create custom image recognition models. Your customers can then find products with ease, thanks to this smart tech. And don't worry, you won't need a computer science degree to use it.

Microsoft's Azure Machine Learning Studio

This platform is like the artist's canvas for AI. It's user-friendly too, with a simple drag-and-drop interface. Let's say you're a content creator or marketer – you can employ Azure's text analytics to understand how your audience feels through sentiment analysis. Plus, it helps with SEO by extracting essential keywords. Want to impress your customers with personalized content recommendations? Azure can do that too!

Start small and work your way up. These tools allow you to run small experiments, like analyzing customer reviews or sorting products by images. As you get the hang of things and see those positive results, you can confidently scale up your AI game.

Google and Microsoft also offer heaps of tutorials and friendly communities eager to help.

Remember, the key to AI success is making it a seamless part of your customer experience. Whether you're enhancing a chatbot's responses or personalizing content, always put your customers' happiness first.

Real-life Success Stories

Often the best way to figure out how to use AI to make money online is to study the most successful online companies. The success of major companies can serve as a valuable source of inspiration and insight for anyone looking to leverage AI to make money online. These companies have demonstrated the immense potential of incorporating AI into their business models. Big players like Amazon, Google, Netflix, Spotify, and Facebook are already leveraging AI in various ways to achieve fantastic success.

By studying how these successful companies have integrated AI into their operations, online entrepreneurs can develop their own strategies on how they might apply AI to enhance their online presence and profitability.

Amazon

Amazon employs a robust AI strategy to enhance customer satisfaction and operational efficiency. One of its key strategies is the implementation of AI-powered recommendation engines. These engines analyze user behavior and preferences, allowing Amazon to offer highly personalized product suggestions. This not only drives higher sales but also fosters customer loyalty. Additionally, Amazon utilizes AI for supply chain optimization, leveraging it to streamline inventory management, demand forecasting, and logistics operations. This results in significant cost savings and improved overall operational efficiency. Furthermore, Amazon employs AI-driven chatbots and virtual assistants to handle customer inquiries in real time. This innovative approach enhances the overall customer experience by providing timely and efficient support.

Google

Google's success hinges on its adept use of AI technologies. One of its pivotal strategies involves the development of algorithms that leverage AI to refine search results and content ranking. This not only heightens user engagement but also drives increased traffic to the platform. Additionally, Google harnesses the power of Natural Language Processing (NLP) to enhance the user experience across its websites, apps, and services. This application of NLP makes these platforms more intuitive and user-friendly, thereby enriching the overall user experience. Moreover, Google applies AI algorithms to optimize advertising campaigns, enabling the targeting of specific demographics with precision. This strategic move substantially improves ad performance, resulting in a higher return on investment for marketing efforts.

Netflix and Spotify

Netflix and Spotify, two industry giants, have recognized the transformative power of AI-driven technologies. By implementing recommendation engines infused with artificial intelligence, they've redefined content suggestions, tailoring movies, music, and shows to individual users. This strategic move not only heightens user retention but also fuels a surge in content consumption. Moreover, an astute analysis of user behavior and preferences unveils the pulse of the audience, pinpointing the most captivating and sought-after content. This treasure trove of data becomes a guiding compass, steering content acquisition and creation strategies toward resonant offerings. The platforms have also honed their approach through AI-powered personalization and customization. This includes crafting a bespoke user interface, curating playlists, and fine-tuning content suggestions to align seamlessly with individual tastes, culminating in an exquisitely tailored user experience.

Facebook

Facebook employs a multifaceted approach to enhance user engagement and experience. Through targeted advertising, the platform leverages AI-driven algorithms to meticulously analyze user data and behavior, enabling the execution of highly precise advertising campaigns. This, in turn, leads to elevated click-through and conversion rates, maximizing the impact of marketing efforts. Additionally, Facebook employs AI for content moderation, effectively identifying and removing inappropriate or violative content, thereby ensuring a safe and engaging user environment. Moreover, the platform harnesses the power of Natural Language Processing (NLP) and translation capabilities to foster inclusivity and expand its global reach. By doing so, Facebook successfully communicates with a broader audience, transcending linguistic barriers.

Remember, emulating large companies doesn't mean copying their exact strategies, but rather understanding the principles they've used. It's important to adapt and customize these approaches to fit your specific industries and target audiences, but the underlying principles of using AI for enhanced user experiences and operational efficiency remain universal.

Practical Advice for Using AI in Online Business

A well-crafted AI strategy should be your compass, pointing the way forward. Whether you already have an established business with an online presence, or just starting out and trying to get into the market by leveraging AI, you'll want to create a plan that ensures long-term sustainability and profitability.

Take the suggested guidelines below and apply them to the unique needs and parameters of your business:

- **Define Clear Objectives and Goals**

   o Determine what you want to achieve with AI in your business. This could be improving customer service, automating processes, enhancing product recommendations, etc.

- **Understand Your Data**

    o Evaluate the quality and quantity of your data. Ensure it's clean, well-structured, and sufficient for AI applications.

- **Identify Use Cases**

    o Identify specific areas where AI can bring the most value. This might be in customer service, marketing, sales, or operations.

- **Select an AI Solution**

    o Decide whether to build custom AI models in-house or use pre-built solutions (like APIs or SaaS platforms). This depends on your budget, expertise, and the complexity of your AI needs.

- **Assemble a Skilled Team**

    o If you're building custom AI solutions for your business, you'll need a team with expertise in machine learning, data science, and software development.

- **Choose the Right Tools and Technologies**

    o Select the platforms, programming languages, frameworks, and libraries that are appropriate for your AI project.

- **Develop and Train Models**

    o Train your AI models based on the use cases you've identified. This is a crucial step in achieving accurate and effective results.

- **Evaluate Model Performance**

    o Use metrics and validation techniques to assess how well your AI models are performing. Make any necessary adjustments to improve accuracy.

- **Integrate AI into Business Processes**

    - Implement the AI solutions into your existing business workflows. This might involve integrating APIs, embedding models, or building custom applications.

- **Test and Validate**

    - Conduct thorough testing to ensure that the integrated AI system functions as expected in real-world scenarios.

- **Monitor and Maintain**

    - Set up monitoring to track the performance of your AI models. Regularly update and retrain models to maintain their accuracy.

- **Compliance and Data Privacy**

    - Ensure that your AI implementation adheres to all relevant data privacy and compliance regulations, such as GDPR or HIPAA.

- **User Training and Adoption**

    - Train your team members on how to effectively use the AI tools and systems in their daily operations.

- **Feedback Loop and Iteration**

    - Establish a feedback loop where users can provide input on the AI system's performance. Use this feedback to make necessary improvements.

- **Scale and Expand**

    - Once you've successfully integrated AI into one area of your business, consider how it can be applied in other departments or processes.

In wrapping up this chapter, remember that your path to online success is uniquely yours to shape. The strategies we've covered are simply tools in a toolbox, ready to be customized to fit your specific goals and audience.

Think of your online venture as a conversation with your audience. What speaks to them? What problems can you solve? These are the questions that will guide you as you adopt AI integration and ensure that it is truly productive and valuable.

What AI Thinks

ChatGPT: *"AI can assist you in making money online by optimizing digital marketing campaigns, identifying profitable niches, and suggesting pricing strategies based on market trends. It can also automate tasks like content generation and customer interactions, allowing you to scale your online business more efficiently. Additionally, AI-powered analytics can provide insights that guide data-driven decision-making, contributing to increased online revenue."*

Chapter 7:

Transforming Real Estate through

Artificial Intelligence

The real estate industry has transformed significantly due to technological advancements and strategic shifts. Initially, transactions were conducted through traditional methods, but the internet changed the game by allowing properties to be listed and searched for online. Online portals and mobile apps made the process even more convenient, providing centralized platforms for buyers and sellers.

With the arrival of AI, the real estate industry has been transformed for efficiency and effectiveness. From monitoring leased or rented properties for regular maintenance alerts, to appraisals and estimates generated through AI-based algorithms, the power of AI and machine learning has enhanced this industry that thrives on data.

Generative AI can also create three-dimensional models of properties so that potential buyers can use any device to get an idea of how the property looks. These can take the form of virtual reality walkthroughs where a buyer can virtually walk into a home and see the property and buildings, or where a model of the building can be generated to see what it looks like before being built.

For real estate agents, utilizing the power of targeted chatbots can significantly enhance the leads of potential buyers and renters. By asking what a client's preferences are and analyzing the relevant information to get to know them better, these AI-powered bots collate clients' data and contact details for future marketing campaigns. This has the effect of cutting down the costs of manual marketing, previously achieved through human interaction.

A recent PwC report estimated that automation and AI are among the top five great disruptors of the real estate industry. Another report suggests that the global generative AI in real estate market size was valued at USD 351.9 million in 2022 and it is projected to reach around USD 1,047 million by 2032.

The Impact of AI on Real Estate

Leveraging AI for Marketing in Real Estate

A great marketing plan in the real estate industry is one that is streamlined and targeted, allowing agents to close deals faster as the pool of potential buyers is geared towards buyers who are not just window shopping.

With the plethora of digital marketing options and platforms available, writing and posting catchy, relevant, and targeted headlines can be time-consuming, costly, and monotonous. However, investing in these platforms is critical to marketing operations as many home buyers can be reached this way.

These AI tools can be specifically trained on information and data from the real estate industry. This helps to generate and suggest posts that would be more successful as the machine learning aspects of AI would have analyzed and sifted through which posts would produce better leads. This takes the leg work of social media research. Companies like Jude AI are designed especially for real estate professionals and have a range of tools to streamline marketing efforts and drive more leads.

Google and Facebook ads can be designed for compelling descriptions to stand out and attract leads, while emails can be generated to enhance the professionalism and persuasiveness of the content. Another aspect of AI is automated responses, where follow-up emails and requests for information can be timely sent so the business does not miss out on opportunities.

These AI-generated marketing campaigns can help a business truly stand out from the noise and elevate a company's focus, providing the management and team with more time to build a superior business and enhance efficiency.

Another powerful AI tool is the Zestimate, which was created by the Zillow Group in Seattle. The company uses machine learning-based neural networks and a multitude of data points in an algorithm created to estimate the market value of a home. Details of the home, location, property tax assessments, and sales histories are just some of the data points used to generate an accurate valuation.

The company has been developing this tool for 15 years and despite the appraisals being estimates, it provides home value data on more than 104 million properties. By tapping into the power of neural networks in machine learning, Zillow can determine prices nationwide through a single network instead of using nearly 1,000 variations of algorithms as it did previously. The error rate, the company says, has also been reduced by almost 12%.

Utilizing AI tools like Zillow's Zestimate has allowed it to scale up its operations and gain a competitive edge, which it can now use to further its vision of bringing the one-click style of e-commerce to the real estate market. This saving on time, scaling up operations, and superior client service was all possible through enhanced machine learning technology.

One other important aspect of how AI tools provide efficiency for both clients and businesses while saving time and money is chatbots.

Real estate chatbots are virtual assistants that can handle inquiries about buying, selling, and renting homes, while also collecting data and scheduling meetings. Squirrel Mortgages from New Zealand uses an AI chatbot called Alan that simulates conversations and answers questions in real-time on its website with people looking for its services.

Chatbots allow a business to streamline its information dissemination and provide clients or potential clients with near-instant responses. Chatbots save time by automating repetitive tasks and keeping track of clients and potential leads. In many cases, chatbots can have an impressive return on investment of over 1000%.

Beyond increasing communication speeds and improving client interactions, AI like ChatGPT can help real estate agents automatically generate catchy and accurate property descriptions. This saves time and ensures listings are attractive to potential buyers.

Streamlining Processes with AI

Automation of administrative tasks is a powerful way in which a business can streamline its operations for efficiency and ultimately success.

In a paper by MIT on the current applications of AI in real estate, the author notes that natural language processing is a powerful tool that allows computers to "read" text and extract pertinent data. Natural language generation gives computers the ability to communicate back to us in "human" terms. These tools are used in real estate-related chatbots, contract review and data extraction, data gathering and processing from text-based sources, and document writing."

Chatbots are significant for a business in more than a marketing sense. Advanced chatbot tools use AI to make major improvements in the office, retail, and industrial leasing environment for small to mid-sized tenants. By collecting data and then guiding the tenant through the leasing process, the reduction of human engagement can speed up the process of business. An example of a Chicago broker was evaluated by the MIT paper and found that one could manage 130 deals compared to a normal brokerage company where four people managed only 30 active deals.

The power of AI extends to visual aspects too, with the real estate profession heavily reliant on images this presents enormous potential for businesses to gain an edge in the market.

Computer vision technology and 3D augmentation can be used to map out an interior virtually. Photographs and videos can be taken of existing buildings and then processed in specialized software like GeoCV, Matterport, Google's ARCore, and others, it generates virtual tours for clients that can provide detailed insights without spending a lot of time and energy on physical tours.

Other uses include generating designs from a pre-defined kit of components with the software able to perform generative design to create the optimal building for each site. This gives building developers the opportunity to understand the impacts of trade-offs that will need to be made in the actual building.

Space planning is an important consideration in construction and to accurately reflect the designs, all considerations must be considered. 3D computer vision that is automatically trained to identify building components and is capable of incredibly detailed analysis can be used to identify construction mistakes and even automate reports to schedule construction of the next steps. Drones that traverse a construction site with lidar and cameras to map out what has been built and how that aligns with the drawings are the power behind this AI technology.

Drones can also be used to give a bird's-eye view of any construction site, while AI overlays can track changes and spot potential geographical issues that may affect building budgets.

Many aspects of the real estate industry can be streamlined with the use of technology before construction and after construction. This enables businesses to save time, money, and focus on more complex tasks while scaling up and growth can happen rapidly.

Future Predictions and Trends

As with anything in technology, and especially now in the age of information and digital data, the race for future technologies is moving at break-neck speed.

With the real estate industry heavily reliant on data points, the value of big data and how it can inform critical decision-making processes will continue to be a trend for the industry.

A McKinsey report on how big data is transforming the real estate industry shows that through advanced analytics using machine learning algorithms "the ability to extract patterns and forecasts and use those predictions to design new market-entry strategies," will be key.

Developers would be able to access use data and market forecasts and select the most relevant neighborhoods and types of buildings for development, including maximizing value by optimizing the timing for development, mix of property uses, and price segmentation.

For asset managers, this type of AI tool can be handy to identify buildings in areas that are undervalued but rising in popularity. While property owners can predict rent and make capital expenditure decisions on specific properties.

Progress in artificial intelligence is frequently exponential rather than linear—and companies must consider them as realistic supplements to their current underwriting, portfolio review, and research processes. If companies fail to act now, they run the risk of adapting too late.

Another area of expansion is automated property valuations, similar to the Zestimate. A recent project by MIT used 27 million street view images across the United States, and was surprised to discover that visual AI is remarkably effective at predicting many aspects of a neighborhood's profile, including poverty, crime, and public health.

Data can be a powerful tool to shape cities and suggests that the Internet of Things (IoT) technologies like sensors and cameras that track and record everything could become commonplace. Mobile phone data can also be powerful in that it can used to track the movement of people, goods, and traffic which in turn could be fed into AI-powered software tools to understand goods flows, social ties, and transportation flows in an effort to design better cities.

From a business-centered point of view, making decisions on construction costs involves hours of research and teams of people to sift through and analyze data gathered. Machine Learning and AI tools can be used to reduce the cost and the time it would take, while in-construction costs can be efficiently managed, tracked, and predicted – like inflationary costs, scarcity of materials, or labor costs. However, sometimes the data points are very tightly guarded and unless anonymized data can be used, this can prove to be difficult.

A platform that uses the principles of data analytics and 3D processes and brings them together may create major efficiencies for estimators, and thus allow real estate professionals to use AI suggestions that make sure the project is completed with the necessary quality control and is within budget.

In the concluding remarks of Conway's paper, the author writes that "technology moves quickly and it may seem difficult to keep up, but if we can see past the excitement of media attention there are plenty of examples of ground-breaking research that is truly opening up insights that never would have been possible before the advent of AI and machine learning."

While these future trends and predictions are not far off, with some already in development, the move to a holistic environment of technology-driven business innovations can come from anywhere. The key is to allow your business the opportunity to experiment and make use of the most valuable technology that is core to business operations. Real estate is one such market that can and does benefit from the plethora of innovations that AI brings.

Challenges and Ethical Considerations

As with all big data in AI-powered applications, bias can perpetuate societal inequalities, affecting decisions related to pricing, lending, and property access. Transparency and accountability are necessary for implementing AI tools responsibly.

The question of who controls and owns this data is of topmost concern. In the face of a lack of regulations, the misuse of this data can have serious consequences for the future of AI but also for the harm it can do to those wishing to exploit the data.

Concerns regarding the privacy of data are also included in the ethical considerations, with businesses encouraged to develop and update policies and procedures governing the use of data.

The concern of algorithmic collusion will become even more stark as AI and machine learning continue to develop and find the best ways for it to reach its objectives. While errors in property valuations can be made, through bias or glitches, these can have severe financial implications for both a company and client. The question of who becomes liable can also take on legal ramifications.

Addressing concerns related to liability, bias, and accountability requires a proactive approach to ensure that AI systems are fair, transparent, and accountable in their decision-making processes.

Integration and Benefits

Integrating AI tools in the real estate market is beginning to mark an era of tremendous benefits, showcasing and catalyzing a remarkable transformation in the industry. These advancements have increased the efficiency of real estate operations while streamlining the experiences of both industry professionals and clients.

One of the most profound advantages of employing AI tools in real estate is its amazing ability to extend market reach. By harnessing the capabilities of data analytics and machine learning algorithms, real estate professionals now have invaluable insights into market dynamics, enabling more informed and strategic decision-making. This newfound AI-assisted understanding allows real estate professionals to create and use precisely targeted marketing strategies, thereby optimizing engagement with potential buyers or tenants. Moreover, AI-driven predictive analytics can pinpoint prospective leads and offer tailor-made recommendations, making closing a deal or sale that much more likely.

Beyond this, AI streamlines the multifaceted processes that are part of the real estate sector. From property valuation to document management and transaction processing, AI solutions trim down the time and effort expended on these tasks. The deployment of virtual assistants and chatbots for handling routine inquiries frees up employees or agents to concentrate on more intricate aspects of their work, resulting in enhanced operations overall. Client satisfaction is a natural progression of this, thanks to the chatbots and other such tools providing rapid, precise responses to inquiries.

Importantly, AI's influence extends into the realms of construction and property management. AI-powered construction technologies like 3D imaging enhance project management and optimize resource allocation and safety protocols, resulting in cost savings and time saved when projects are completed faster.

Practical Steps to Include AI in Your Real Estate Business Strategy

It may seem daunting to consider changing your existing business strategy and incorporating AI but the benefits hugely outweigh the costs. To make things easier consider following the steps below to ensure you get the most out of AI:

- **Research and Education**

    o Familiarize yourself and your team with AI technologies and their applications in real estate.

    o Understand the benefits and potential drawbacks of using AI in your business.

- **Identify Pain Points and Objectives**

    o Determine specific areas in your real estate business where AI can add value, such as lead generation, property valuation, customer service, etc.

    o Set clear objectives for what you want to achieve with AI implementation.

- **Data Collection and Cleaning**

    o Gather relevant data related to your real estate operations (property listings, customer data, market trends, etc.).

    o Clean and organize the data to ensure it's suitable for machine learning applications.

- **Select AI Use Cases**

  - Choose specific AI applications that align with your objectives and address identified pain points.

  - Examples include predictive analytics for property prices, chatbots for customer service, or image recognition for property evaluation.

- **Choose AI Tools and Platforms**

  - Select appropriate AI tools or platforms based on your chosen use cases. Consider factors like cost, compatibility, and ease of integration.

- **Develop or Acquire AI Models**

  - Depending on your resources, you can either develop custom AI models or use pre-built models from established providers. This could involve hiring AI experts or using AI-as-a-service platforms.

- **Integration with Existing Systems**

  - Ensure that the chosen AI solutions integrate smoothly with your existing software and databases. This might require custom development or using APIs.

- **Compliance and Data Security**

  - Ensure that you are compliant with data privacy regulations (such as GDPR or CCPA) and that sensitive information is handled securely.

- **Training and Testing**

  - Train your AI models using the prepared data and fine-tune them for optimal performance.

  - Test the models rigorously to ensure accuracy, reliability, and efficiency.

- **Deployment and Monitoring**

  - Implement AI solutions in your real estate operations. Monitor their performance closely to identify any issues or improvements that may be needed.

- **User Training and Adoption**

  - Train your team on how to effectively use and interact with the AI tools. Encourage adoption and provide ongoing support.

- **Feedback Loop and Iteration**

  - Establish a feedback loop where your team can report issues and suggest improvements for the AI systems. Use this feedback to iterate and refine the models.

- **Measure ROI and Performance**

  - Evaluate the return on investment of your AI implementation by tracking metrics like increased lead generation, improved customer satisfaction, or cost savings.

- **Scale and Expand**

  - Once the initial AI systems are successfully implemented, consider expanding their use to other areas of your real estate business or exploring additional AI applications.

As we reflect on the manifold benefits AI brings to the real estate industry, it is vital to recognize that this technology continues to evolve. Remember that implementing AI in a real estate business is an ongoing process that requires ongoing learning, maintenance, and adaptation.

In the upcoming chapter, we will delve into the dynamic arena of social media marketing, another transformative element that promises to further reshape the real estate landscape. With social media marketing, real estate professionals are empowered to leverage the immense reach and influence of social platforms, revolutionizing the way properties are promoted and connecting with a broader audience.

What AI Thinks

ChatGPT: "AI transforms real estate marketing by providing personalized property recommendations, predicting market trends, and enabling immersive virtual tours. It enhances customer interaction through chatbots, automates content generation, and offers data-driven insights for targeted marketing strategies. AI also optimizes ad campaigns, analyzes local market trends, and assists in property valuation, revolutionizing how real estate professionals connect with buyers and promote properties."

Chapter 8:

Enhancing Social Media Marketing

Using Artificial Intelligence

After seeing how AI can be plugged into almost any business niche, you might be asking yourself what else is possible with AI?

In the same way that the automobile replaced the wagon, AI is making our world move faster. But it has had more than just a technological effect on our society, the world of marketing has also been revamped.

We've come a long way. In the early years of marketing, businesses relied on traditional mediums such as television, print, and radio to reach a broad audience. The challenge lies in tailoring messages to diverse consumer segments.

Then the emergence of the internet revolutionized advertising practices. Companies quickly recognized the potential of websites as virtual storefronts, opening up new channels for customer interaction. Email marketing gained prominence as a direct line of communication, while search engines introduced concepts like SEO and PPC advertising. The internet provided a platform for global reach, but the challenge remained, how could we personalize marketing interactions for diverse audiences?

With social media, the focus shifted towards content marketing. Valuable, relevant content became the currency of the digital realm. Brands transitioned from one-way advertising to creating narratives that resonated with their audience. This shift required a deeper understanding of customer preferences and behaviors, driving the need for data-driven insights and analytics.

As marketers tried to leverage big data and analytics to personalize their messages and offers, the customer experience became paramount. Companies struggled to meet expectations and provide seamless interactions across multiple touchpoints. Until AI joined the ranks that is.

AI's role in social media marketing is nothing short of revolutionary. It's here to make your life easier and your marketing campaigns more effective. Imagine having a tireless assistant who not only automates a wide range of tasks but also has the ability to process vast amounts of data, offering you invaluable insights about your content and your audience. It will completely transform your marketing game.

What really sets AI apart in social media marketing is its incredible adaptability and algorithmic brilliance. It can learn from user behavior, recognize patterns, and swiftly adjust its tactics. with all of this backed by data-driven decision-making. With AI by your side, you can laser-focus your efforts on specific demographics, delivering tailor-made content that resonates with your target audience in remarkable ways.

Different Types of AI Tools

Whether you want to refine your content strategy, optimize posting schedules, or receive personalized creative suggestions, integrating Artificial Intelligence into your social media toolkit can be a game-changer. And there is a literal plethora of AI tools to use in marketing.

Incorporating Artificial Intelligence into social media marketing represents a quantum leap in the way your audience engages with your business. By harnessing the power of AI, marketers can refine targeting, optimize content, improve customer service, and stay ahead of trends. It is versatile and can be implemented in a number of methods to suit your approach to marketing.

Customer Segmentation and Targeting

AI empowers marketers to refine their audience targeting. Through data analysis and machine learning, AI algorithms can identify patterns in user behavior, preferences, and demographics. This information helps create highly segmented and personalized campaigns, ensuring that content reaches the right people at the right time.

Content Optimization

AI tools like Natural Language Processing and computer vision enhance content creation and curation. NLP enables the analysis of text data, enabling businesses to understand customer sentiments, preferences, and feedback. Computer vision, on the other hand, allows for the interpretation of visual content, making it easier to identify trends and create engaging visuals.

Ad Campaign Optimization

AI-driven algorithms can optimize advertising campaigns for maximum impact. They continuously analyze performance data, adjusting targeting parameters, ad formats, and budgets in real time to maximize ROI.

Social Listening and Sentiment Analysis

AI-powered tools can monitor social media platforms for brand mentions, keywords, and sentiments. This enables businesses to gain real-time feedback, identify potential issues, and respond promptly, thus enhancing their online reputation.

The Power of Chatbots

A huge element of AI in marketing is the rise of the Chatbots. Utilizing these in your marketing strategy is a way to hugely advance your customer engagement.

Specifically by providing real-time, automated customer engagement. They're available 24/7, ensuring that inquiries are promptly addressed, which builds trust and enhances customer satisfaction.

These AI-powered agents come equipped with Natural Language Processing capabilities, allowing them to understand and respond to user queries in a conversational manner. They can offer instant answers to frequently asked questions, guide users through troubleshooting, and even assist in completing transactions.

One of the major advantages of chatbots is their scalability and efficiency. They can handle multiple conversations simultaneously, ensuring that even during high-traffic periods, no customer is left unattended. This scalability is especially crucial for businesses with a large customer base.

From a cost perspective, chatbots are a highly cost-effective solution for customer support. They eliminate the need for hiring and training a large team of agents. This cost-saving is particularly beneficial for startups and small businesses looking to optimize their resources.

Chatbots can provide a personalized customer experience by recognizing returning customers and tailoring responses based on past interactions. They can recommend products or services based on individual preferences, creating a tailored experience that resonates with customers.

Beyond customer support, chatbots excel in lead qualification and generation. They can be programmed to gather information about potential customers, their preferences, and specific needs. This data can then be used to segment leads for targeted marketing efforts.

Chatbots are also valuable data collection tools. They gather insights about customer behavior, preferences, and pain points. This data can be analyzed to refine marketing strategies, improve products or services, and enhance overall customer experience.

Customers today expect quick responses on social media platforms, and chatbots excel in this aspect by providing instantaneous replies. This reduces customer frustration and increases the likelihood of conversion.

Language and location flexibility are additional advantages of chatbots. They can communicate in multiple languages, breaking down language barriers and expanding a business's global reach. Additionally, they can provide location-specific information or services, catering to a diverse and geographically dispersed customer base.

Lastly, chatbots seamlessly integrate with Customer Relationship Management (CRM) systems, ensuring that customer interactions and data are recorded. This information can be used to nurture leads, track customer history, and personalize future interactions, further enhancing the effectiveness of social media marketing efforts.

Predictive Analytics in Action

In chapter 3 we touched on predictive analytics while championing AI's utility as an investment management tool. Unsurprisingly, it is also a cornerstone of modern social media marketing, harnessing data and advanced algorithms to forecast forthcoming trends and consumer behavior. By scrutinizing historical data, it discerns patterns and extrapolates insights, enabling businesses to anticipate shifts in consumer preferences, content engagement, and purchasing behavior. This foresight empowers marketers to adapt content strategies proactively, creating more resonant and relevant material. Furthermore, predictive analytics refines audience segmentation, allowing for precision targeting based on the characteristics and behaviors of high-value customers. This results in higher conversion rates and a more effective allocation of resources.

In product development, predictive analytics guides innovation by illuminating anticipated features or offerings in demand, allowing businesses to outpace the competition and deliver products that align with evolving consumer needs. Ad campaigns also benefit from this tool, as it forecasts demographic responses, enabling businesses to optimize resources and maximize return on investment. Moreover, predictive analytics provides the means to anticipate customer needs, fostering proactive provision of products or services, and ultimately enhancing customer satisfaction and loyalty.

Beyond the immediate returns, predictive analytics contributes to long-term success. It aids in identifying indicators of potential customer attrition, enabling businesses to implement retention strategies in a timely manner. Additionally, you can use it to adjust your strategic planning around seasonal trends and events, ensuring marketing efforts align with periods of heightened demand.

The power of predictive analytics lies in its continuous refinement. As new data emerges, models evolve, and predictions become increasingly accurate. This adaptability equips businesses to navigate a dynamic market landscape with agility and responsiveness.

In sum, predictive analytics is indispensable for social media marketers seeking to not only keep pace with change but also stay ahead of it. It empowers them to make well-informed decisions, optimize strategies, and engage effectively with their audience in this ever-evolving digital race.

Image Recognition

Image recognition technology has a significant impact on social media marketing. It goes beyond just accessibility, making user experiences much smoother.

Image recognition also plays a crucial role in maintaining a secure online space. It quickly identifies and flags inappropriate content, which is especially important for platforms with strict content guidelines.

Personalization becomes possible with image recognition as it understands users' visual preferences, providing tailored content recommendations. This leads to higher engagement and stronger user retention. In terms of user-generated content, image recognition helps brands find authentic material for their marketing efforts.

Image recognition empowers businesses with valuable competitor analysis. By understanding competitors' visual content strategies, you gain a competitive edge. Additionally, brand sentiment analysis allows you to see how your brand is visually perceived, helping you make necessary adjustments for optimal impact.

For e-commerce platforms, image recognition can revolutionize the shopping experience by quickly identifying and tagging products within images. And when it comes to augmented reality integration, image recognition truly stands out. It offers interactive and engaging content based on real-world objects or images, creating an immersive experience for potential customers.

Using image recognition for trend identification is a powerful tool for marketers, allowing them to create content that truly resonates with their target audience. As this technology continues to evolve, its impact on social media marketing is set to expand, offering innovative ways to engage users and boost brand visibility in an increasingly visual digital landscape.

Examples of successful image recognition integration can be found in various platforms, with standout instances in services such as Pinterest and Google Photos. These platforms have adeptly incorporated image recognition technology, showcasing its remarkable potential to revolutionize user experiences and propel, brand success.

Pinterest, for instance, has harnessed image recognition to create a seamless and intuitive browsing experience. By employing advanced algorithms, Pinterest can accurately identify objects, colors, and styles within images, allowing users to effortlessly discover related content and products. This not only keeps users engaged for longer durations but also significantly boosts the platform's conversion rates.

Likewise, Google Photos exemplifies the power of image recognition in organizing and managing vast collections of photographs. Through cutting-edge machine learning models, Google Photos can automatically tag and categorize images, making them easily searchable and retrievable. This feature not only saves users valuable time but also deepens their connection with the platform, as they can effortlessly revisit cherished memories.

These visual giants showcase how image recognition technology has evolved beyond a mere novelty, becoming an indispensable tool for optimizing user interactions and fostering brand loyalty. By taking advantage of AI's innovative capabilities, companies can forge more meaningful connections with their audience, ultimately leading to enhanced customer satisfaction and business growth.

Practical Tips to Incorporate AI in Your Strategy

Imagine having a digital companion that not only excels at crunching numbers and unveiling the secrets of your audience's preferences but also knows precisely when they're most active online. With this AI wingman by your side, you can bid farewell to the age-old guessing game and say hello to content that fits your audience like a tailor-made suit.

AI also possesses the remarkable ability to transform your visuals into true works of art. It's like having a personal graphic designer who never needs a coffee refill. The precision and creativity it brings to your visual content are unmatched, ensuring that your brand stands out in a crowded digital landscape.

And let's not forget about those AI-driven chatbots, the unsung heroes of customer support. They're always ready to tackle queries and guide potential customers to your virtual doorstep. With their round-the-clock availability and instant responses, you can provide top-notch support and turn potential leads into loyal customers effortlessly.

In essence, with AI as your ally, you're not just keeping up with the times – you're setting the pace, revolutionizing the way you engage with your audience, and leaving a lasting impression in the digital sphere.

While it might seem hard to suddenly convert your marketing strategy and incorporate AI into it, here are a few things that you can keep in mind as you consider using AI in your social media marketing:

- **Set Clear Objectives**

  o Define specific goals for using AI in your social media marketing efforts, such as improving customer engagement or optimizing ad performance.

- **Select Relevant AI Tools**

  o Choose AI platforms or tools that align with your objectives, such as chatbots for customer engagement or recommender systems for content personalization.

- **Collect and Organize Data**

  o Ensure you have access to relevant data from your social media platforms. This data will be essential for AI-driven insights and recommendations.

- **Implement Chatbots**

  o Integrate chatbots to provide instant responses to customer inquiries and guide users through simple transactions. They enhance customer service and engagement.

- **Utilize Recommender Systems**

  o Leverage AI-powered recommender systems to suggest personalized content to your audience, based on their preferences and behavior.

- **Optimize Ad Campaigns with AI**

  o Make use of AI-driven features in advertising platforms to maximize the ROI of your ad campaigns through automated targeting and bidding.

- **Monitor, Analyze, and Iterate**

  o Continuously assess the performance of AI-driven features. Analyze the data to refine your strategies and adapt to emerging trends in AI and social media marketing.

The integration of AI into your social media marketing is not just a wise choice; it's a leap toward success in our ever-transforming digital landscape. As we've delved deeper, you've likely discovered the incredible potential of AI tools to revolutionize your practical strategies, from automating routine tasks to uncovering invaluable insights about your audience.

Why is it such a brilliant idea to embrace AI in your social media marketing efforts? Well, because it empowers you to achieve more with less. By setting clear objectives and harnessing the right AI tools, you'll find yourself navigating the intricate world of social media marketing with newfound agility and precision. This isn't about replacing humans in marketing, it is about freeing up your time to focus on what truly matters—engaging with your audience, understanding your clients, and nurturing your brand's unique voice.

Another relevant creative task is AI-driven content and copywriting. From generating persuasive product descriptions to crafting personalized email campaigns, AI is your steadfast ally in the quest for digital marketing excellence. We'll dig into this industry as well.

So take heart and embrace the AI-powered revolution. With the right strategies and tools, your social media marketing campaigns will soar to new heights. The future is bright, and your potential is limitless. The journey continues, and it's filled with promise and innovation.

What AI Thinks

ChatGPT: "AI revolutionizes social media marketing by analyzing user behavior to tailor content, optimize posting times, and enhance engagement. It automates content creation, suggests trending topics, and manages ad campaigns for maximum reach and impact. AI-driven insights provide data-driven strategies that enable marketers to connect with their target audience effectively and drive successful social media campaigns."

Chapter 9:

Utilizing Artificial Intelligence to Enhance Your Writing Process

We've ventured through other industries and witnessed AI's responsible deployment in the pursuit of profit and efficiency. It's remarkable how AI seamlessly finds its place in almost every conceivable scenario. You might be forgiven at this stage if you think that AI is only useful for analytics, crunching numbers, and chatting to clients.

Now we step into a field where AI might be poised to deliver some of its most remarkable utility. The world of writing.

Over the last half-century, the writing industry has undergone significant transformations, largely driven by technological advancements and shifts in publishing practices.

In the earlier years, traditional publishing houses held a dominant position. Authors typically required literary agents to secure publishing deals, making it a somewhat exclusive arena. However, diversity in both authors and content was limited, with established voices often taking precedence.

The advent of personal computers and word processing software in the late 20th century democratized the writing process. This accessibility broadened the field, allowing a wider audience to engage in writing. Additionally, authors gained the ability to self-publish through print-on-demand services, albeit in a relatively niche manner.

The turn of the millennium brought about a digital revolution. E-books gained prominence, challenging the dominance of print books. Online retailers provided platforms for self-publishing, leading to the rise of independent authors. Simultaneously, the internet became a fertile ground for blogging and online content creation, enabling writers to reach global audiences directly.

It's here that we'll find a truly compelling partnership between human creativity and machine intelligence.

In writing, AI becomes a keen collaborator rather than a mere tool. It doesn't just correct grammatical errors; it redefines the writing process, elevating it to new heights. Writers, across various genres and disciplines, now have a broad spectrum of AI-powered tools at their disposal, designed not only to save time but also to enhance the quality of their work and unlock fresh creative possibilities.

Picture it as a harmonious dance between human ingenuity and AI's algorithmic precision. This synergy transcends conventional boundaries, reshaping the writing landscape. In this chapter, we embark on a discussion about how AI, particularly NLP, is revolutionizing the art of writing. It's a journey into the future where wordsmiths work with machines to craft a narrative that seamlessly blends human thought with computational prowess.

Understanding AI Tools for Writers

Artificial Intelligence is a formidable ally when it comes to writing, offering a suite of capabilities that can revolutionize the creative process. So understanding the basics of these AI writing tools should be your priority.

To begin with, there are two key areas you should focus on. The first is text generation, where AI can swiftly produce customized written content with impressive accuracy.

Second is using AI as a meticulous editor, who can correct grammar and style; and polish your work to a high standard.

The best way to view AI is as a complementary force to human creativity and expertise. By understanding the depth of its capabilities you can harness its power to enhance your productivity without sacrificing the essence of your unique voice and storytelling prowess. This synergy between human ingenuity and AI capabilities lets technology augment, rather than replace, the creative process.

Creative Idea Generation with AI

AI's ability to generate creative ideas is a valuable asset for writers. It offers a wellspring of inspiration and can be a catalyst for exploring new narrative avenues, ultimately leading to more imaginative and engaging writing.

There is a great story for aspiring authors who are seeking to revolutionize their creative writing process:

Author Tim Boucher leveraged AI-powered tools to craft a staggering 97 books, a feat that would typically span years for conventional writers. His impressive turnaround time ranges from an astonishing three hours for one book, to a maximum of eight.

Key to Boucher's literary journey is the utilization of ChatGPT, powered by the cutting-edge GPT-4, alongside Anthropic's Claude for brainstorming and text generation. For visual inspiration, he employed the AI image generator MidJourney, which breathed life into his narratives.

Boucher embarked on this transformative endeavor in August 2022. From August to May of the next year, his literary creations found eager readers, resulting in the sale of 574 books and earnings of approximately $2,000.

Ideation Utility

Before you jump in trying to copy Boucher and end up getting lost in the huge selection of AI tools that are available, here are a few practical tips to approach using AI in effective idea generation for your writing:

- **Prompt Generation**

  - AI models like ChatGPT-3.5 are adept at generating prompts and ideas for various genres and topics. They can provide a starting point for a story, article, or poem, sparking your imagination.

- **Divergent Thinking**

  - AI can offer unconventional and diverse ideas that may not have occurred to you initially. This can lead to more innovative and unique content.

- **Genre Exploration**

  - AI can suggest ideas in different genres or styles, encouraging writers to step out of their comfort zones and explore new creative territories.

- **Combining Concepts**

  - AI can synthesize multiple concepts or elements into a single idea, leading to novel and unexpected combinations that can fuel creativity.

- **Tailored Suggestions**

  - Some AI models can be fine-tuned to mimic the style of a specific author or genre. This allows for personalized idea generation that aligns with the writer's preferences and goals.

- **Visual Prompts**

  - AI can generate descriptions or narratives based on visual inputs, such as images or scenes. This can be a powerful tool for visual artists looking to translate images into words.

- **Interactive Storytelling**

  - AI-powered systems can engage in interactive storytelling, where the writer can input choices, and AI generates the corresponding narrative. This can lead to dynamic and engaging storylines.

- **World Building and Setting Creation**

  - AI can help in the creation of detailed settings, worlds, or environments for fiction writers, providing a rich backdrop for their narratives.

- **Character Development**

  - AI can assist in brainstorming character traits, backstories, and motivations, helping writers create well-rounded and compelling characters.

- **Enhancing Existing Ideas**

  - AI can take a basic concept and suggest ways to expand, refine, or add depth to it, providing a fresh perspective on existing ideas.

- **Cultural and Historical Insights**

  - AI can provide information and insights about different cultures, time periods, or places, enriching the authenticity and depth of a writer's work.

These are just a few of the many ways that AI can boost your creativity as a writer. However it can offer far more than just color and flair to your words, it can also help you overcome some of the major pitfalls in writing and storytelling.

Overcoming Writers' Block

If you've ever tried to write any substantial amount of content, you've probably run into moments where you feel like you've hit a wall.

Writer's block is a common condition that many writers encounter at some point in their creative journey. It refers to a prolonged period of creative stagnation, where the flow of ideas and the ability to produce new work comes to a standstill. This can be an incredibly frustrating and discouraging experience, leaving writers feeling stuck and unable to make progress on their projects.

This phenomenon can take various forms, ranging from struggling to find the right words or ideas, to a complete lack of motivation to write. It's not limited to any particular genre or level of experience; writers of all backgrounds and expertise can be affected.

There are several underlying factors that can contribute to writer's block. Perfectionism, for example, often plays a significant role. The fear of producing anything less than perfect work can create mental barriers that hinder the writing process. Similarly, self-doubt can lead to a lack of confidence, making it difficult to put pen to paper.

Another common cause is overwhelm. Faced with a large or complex project, writers may feel uncertain about where to start, leading to a sense of paralysis. External pressures, such as deadlines or expectations from publishers, editors, or even oneself, can also create stress and mental blocks.

At times, a lack of clear inspiration can be a major hurdle. Without a concrete idea to build upon, starting or continuing a writing project can be a daunting task. Additionally, burnout or fatigue, both mentally and emotionally, can significantly impact creativity and productivity.

Even the monotony of sticking to rigid routines or approaches to writing can lead to a lack of novelty and creative stimulation.

This is where AI can step in as a versatile tool. It provides writers with the support and guidance needed to overcome these initial hurdles. By offering suggestions, generating ideas, and even assisting in the editing process, AI can help writers regain their creative momentum and confidence in their craft.

There are numerous AI websites, apps, and extensions that you can utilize when struggling with writer's block. These range from chatting with ChatGPT to using Dibbly Create for research and style suggestions.

Improving Editing and Proofreading Processes

One cannot talk about AI in literature without highlighting the editorial power of AI tools. AI tools are becoming invaluable for editorial and proofreading purposes in writing. They excel at rectifying grammatical errors, punctuation issues, and spelling mistakes, ensuring that the writing is polished and error-free.

Additionally, they maintain consistent style and tone throughout a piece, offering suggestions for uniformity in language and formatting. These tools analyze sentence structure, providing recommendations for enhanced clarity, coherence, and flow, particularly beneficial for refining complex or awkwardly constructed sentences.

Furthermore, they enrich vocabulary by suggesting synonyms or alternative word choices, elevating the overall quality of writing.

AI can also detect potential instances of plagiarism, preserving originality and academic integrity. It aids in adhering to specific style guides and ensuring proper formatting and citations. Additionally, it evaluates the readability of a piece, offering suggestions to enhance comprehension for the intended audience. With the ability to identify shifts in verb tense, and inconsistencies in voice usage, and eliminate redundant phrases, AI significantly streamlines the editing process. Advanced models can understand context and provide more nuanced suggestions based on specific content and writing styles.

While AI tools greatly expedite the editing and proofreading process, they should complement rather than replace human judgment and creativity, as they may not always capture subtle nuances or context-dependent decisions.

The leader in this field is Grammarly, which has numerous customizable settings to match the language and style that you want to write in. However, there are multiple ways that you can utilize AI to analyze and improve your writing during the editorial process.

If you use any kind of writing platform to capture your content, you are probably already using a number of AI tools without even realizing it. In a way, even Microsoft Word's spellcheck is essentially an AI tool.

An interesting author who successfully utilized AI to both create and edit their writing is Stephen Marche. Marche wrote a stunning and controversial novel titled "Death of an Author" which follows the murder mystery of an author who ironically also uses AI.

He employed three AI programs to draw out the story from his laptop. Initially, using ChatGPT, he developed an outline of the plot, along with a plethora of prompts and notes.

He then used the other two, Sudowrite and Cohere, to edit his word choice and sentence structure, adjust style and tone, and develop the dialogue and descriptive prose of the manuscript.

Tips to Start Writing with AI

It is easier than you think to get started on writing with AI. Blending AI into your writing process can be a great way to enhance creativity, productivity, and efficiency. Here's a step-by-step chronological list to get you started:

- **Define Your Writing Goals and Needs**
    - Determine the specific areas where you want to leverage AI. For example, generating ideas, improving grammar, creating content, etc.

- **Research AI Writing Tools**
    - Explore various AI-powered writing tools and platforms available in the market. Consider factors like capabilities,

user reviews, pricing, and compatibility with your preferred writing environment.

- **Select a Suitable AI Tool**

  - Based on your research, choose an AI writing tool that aligns with your writing goals and budget. Some popular options include OpenAI's GPT-3 (or newer versions, if available), Grammarly, and other specialized writing tools like Quillbot or Dibbly Create.

- **Familiarize Yourself with the Tool**

  - Take some time to learn how to use the selected AI writing tool. Read through tutorials, watch videos, and experiment with the tool to get comfortable with its features and capabilities.

- **Integrate AI into Your Writing Process**

  - Start by incorporating AI at specific stages of your writing process. For example:

    - Idea Generation: Use AI to brainstorm ideas or prompts for your writing projects.

    - Drafting: Experiment with AI-generated content to kickstart your writing or to help overcome writer's block.

    - Editing and Proofreading: Leverage AI tools for grammar and style checks.

- **Experiment and Iterate**

  - Test different approaches to using AI in your writing process. Experiment with using AI for different types of content, such as articles, blog posts, fiction, etc. Adjust your workflow based on what works best for you.

- **Customize AI Outputs**

  o Many AI writing tools allow for customization. Explore settings or options that enable you to fine-tune the output to match your writing style and preferences.

- **Review and Revise AI-Generated Content**

  o While AI can provide a valuable starting point, it's important to review and revise the content it generates. Ensure that it aligns with your vision and intended message.

- **Maintain a Balance**

  o Use AI as a supplement to your creativity and skills, not a replacement. Remember that your unique voice and perspective are what make your writing special.

- **Seek Feedback**

  o Share your AI-assisted writing with trusted peers or writing groups. Gather feedback on how effectively the AI tool is helping you achieve your writing goals.

- **Reflect and Adapt**

  o Regularly assess how incorporating AI is impacting your writing process. Adjust your approach based on what is working best for you.

Embracing AI in your writing endeavors is akin to discovering an invaluable treasure trove of creativity and efficiency. It doesn't seek to supplant your distinctive voice, but rather, it empowers it with an unparalleled surge of potential. With AI by your side, ideas flow freely, sentences shimmer with finesse, and those editing hurdles become a breeze.

AI offers incredible benefits for writers, especially in areas like idea generation, grammar and style enhancement, content research, translation, and time-saving editing. By leveraging these AI capabilities, writers can enhance their productivity and the quality of their work.

Always bear in mind that the key lies in discovering the tools and techniques that resonate most profoundly with your own style and process. In doing so, you unlock a realm of possibilities that could redefine your writing journey. The next breakthrough, the turning point in your narrative, might just be a few keystrokes and clicks away.

With a rich and vibrant future ahead of us, AI is here to stay. Getting cozy with AI writing tools sooner rather than later will give you a serious edge, both as a content creator and a thriving business. So, why not dive in and be prepared?

What AI Thinks

ChatGPT: "AI transforms the writing process by generating content, proofreading, and providing language translation services. It can produce articles, blog posts, and product descriptions based on input parameters and topics. AI writing tools assist in creating high-quality, consistent, and diverse content across various platforms, saving time and expanding creative possibilities."

Chapter 10:

Future Predictions for Artificial

Intelligence

Through ongoing breakthroughs in research, the boundaries of what AI can achieve will continue to be pushed. This constant evolution will drive innovation and open new avenues for application, shaping a future where AI plays an even more central role in our lives and industries. Staying informed and updated with current developments in the field will be crucial as AI's role is set to expand and evolve in ways that have the potential to redefine various aspects of society and our daily lives.

If you don't stay updated with AI developments, you might miss out on important progress in technology. This could lead to inefficiencies, security risks, and a lack of competitive advantage. You might also struggle to innovate and adapt to changing industries. Understanding AI is increasingly important for job opportunities, ethical considerations, and legal compliance. Additionally, staying informed allows you to participate in discussions about AI's impact on society and seize potential collaboration opportunities. It's not about becoming an expert, but about being aware of major trends to make informed decisions in our rapidly changing technological world.

Let's jump into some predictions about what AI is likely to look like in the near future.

Predictions about AI's Future Role

In the future, AI is poised to play a multifaceted role that spans various industries and sectors. An overarching theme will be the heightened emphasis on ethical and responsible AI development, ensuring that systems are fair, transparent, and accountable. This commitment to ethical AI will underpin its integration into key sectors such as healthcare, finance, education, and cybersecurity. In healthcare, AI will continue to revolutionize medical imaging, drug discovery, and personalized medicine, while in finance, it will bolster fraud detection, risk assessment, and customer service.

This seamless fusion of AI and automation is set to become even more prevalent, with robotics being a major beneficiary. This integration will usher in a new era of automation across industries like manufacturing, logistics, and transportation, fundamentally transforming the way these sectors operate. In parallel, the evolution of Natural Language Processing will lead to expanded applications, ranging from more sophisticated chatbots to advanced translation services and sentiment analysis.

Beyond practical applications, AI's creative potential is also set to flourish, influencing realms like music, art, writing, and design. These AI-generated creations will likely become increasingly integrated into our cultural landscape. As these advancements surge forward, governments and organizations are expected to play a pivotal role in shaping AI's trajectory through the implementation of policies and regulations that guide responsible development and use. This will not only ensure that AI benefits society as a whole but also mitigate potential risks and challenges.

As AI continues to evolve, its impact on the employment landscape will be a dynamic interplay. While some roles may be automated, new opportunities requiring collaboration between humans and AI will emerge. This shift in employment dynamics will necessitate adaptability and reskilling, marking a significant societal transformation. Additionally, AI's potential for social good will be increasingly harnessed to address critical issues such as healthcare disparities and poverty alleviation, further cementing its role as a force for positive change.

Impact on Industries

Overall, AI will be a transformative force, impacting nearly every industry. It will drive efficiency, innovation, and new opportunities, but it will also require careful consideration of ethical, regulatory, and societal implications.

The impact of AI on various industries will be profound and wide-ranging here are a few of the most likely developments to come in the near and far future for AI:

- Healthcare: AI will revolutionize healthcare through improved diagnostic accuracy, personalized treatment plans, and enhanced patient care. Medical imaging, drug discovery, and disease prediction will see significant advancements.

- Finance: In the financial sector, AI will bolster fraud detection, risk assessment, and customer service. It will also enable more accurate investment strategies and optimize financial operations.

- Education: AI-powered personalized learning experiences will become more prevalent, adapting teaching methods to individual student needs. Additionally, educational tools using AI will enhance the learning process.

- Manufacturing and Logistics: Integration of AI with robotics will lead to more efficient and flexible manufacturing processes. In logistics, AI will optimize supply chain management, leading to cost savings and improved delivery times.

- Cybersecurity: AI will play a crucial role in identifying and mitigating cybersecurity threats. It will enable real-time threat detection and response, enhancing overall digital security.

- Retail and E-Commerce: AI-driven recommendation systems will provide more personalized shopping experiences. Inventory management, demand forecasting, and customer service will also benefit from AI applications.

- Entertainment and Media: AI will contribute to content creation in music, art, writing, and design. Personalized content recommendations and targeted advertising will become more sophisticated.

- Energy and Sustainability: AI will optimize energy consumption, improve grid management, and contribute to the development of sustainable energy solutions. It will also play a role in addressing environmental challenges.

- Automotive and Transportation: The advent of autonomous vehicles will reshape the automotive industry. AI will also enhance safety features, optimize traffic management, and improve overall transportation efficiency.

- Legal and Compliance: AI will assist in legal research, document review, and contract analysis, leading to more efficient legal processes. It will also help ensure regulatory compliance.

- Real Estate and Construction: AI will streamline property management, optimize construction processes, and improve building efficiency through smart systems.

- Agriculture: AI-driven precision agriculture will optimize crop yields, reduce resource usage, and enhance overall farm management.

- Hospitality and Tourism: AI-powered chatbots and virtual assistants will enhance customer service and improve booking experiences in the hospitality industry. Personalized recommendations for travelers will also become more sophisticated.

- Government and Public Services: AI will be used for tasks like data analysis, predictive policing, and optimizing public service operations, leading to more efficient and effective governance.

- Non-Profit and Social Impact: AI will be harnessed to address critical societal challenges such as healthcare disparities, poverty alleviation, and environmental conservation.

The DeepMind Health Project

A great showcase of the ways that AI can impact business and data handling is the DeepMind Health Project. Before being absorbed into Google Health, DeepMind Health was a division of DeepMind Technologies, a British artificial intelligence company.

One of the standout applications of AI in this project was the development of the mobile app called Streams. Streams utilized advanced machine learning algorithms to assist clinicians in monitoring patients with acute kidney injury (AKI). By employing AI-driven algorithms, the app could provide timely alerts to healthcare providers and grant them access to critical clinical information.

The integration of AI in Streams aimed to enhance the speed and accuracy of patient care, potentially saving lives through early detection and intervention. By automating the analysis of patient data and generating actionable insights, AI played a pivotal role in transforming the way healthcare professionals interacted with and managed patient information.

It's worth noting that the introduction of AI in healthcare also raised important ethical and privacy considerations. The DeepMind project faced scrutiny regarding the handling and sharing of patient data. In 2017, the Information Commissioner's Office in the UK ruled that the Royal Free NHS Trust, a partner in the project, had not fully complied with data protection laws in providing patient data to DeepMind.

This brings us full circle to once again face the ethical impacts of AI implementation in any industry.

Ethical Considerations

Several pivotal considerations will significantly influence the trajectory of ethical AI development and deployment.

Foremost, the pursuit of fairness and the mitigation of biases will be essential, ensuring that AI systems yield equitable outcomes across various contexts. Transparency and explainability will play a central role, demanding that AI processes and decisions become more comprehensible and justifiable. As AI systems evolve, achieving a balance between privacy and data protection will remain a critical principle, safeguarding individuals' sensitive information. Accountability and responsibility will gain prominence, necessitating the establishment of clear lines of ownership for AI-generated actions.

Furthermore, defining the boundaries of human-AI collaboration will be a critical focal point, ensuring that AI systems serve as complements to human capabilities rather than replacements. Ethical frameworks for autonomous systems and their decision-making processes will need to be established, particularly in domains like autonomous vehicles and healthcare, where AI's autonomy becomes more prevalent. The principle of beneficence will guide efforts to harness AI for the betterment of humanity, emphasizing positive societal impacts across a spectrum of industries and applications.

Addressing the long-term implications and potential risks associated with advanced AI will be an ongoing ethical consideration, as society grapples with the broader ramifications of these technologies. Setting ethical boundaries for dual-use scenarios, where AI technologies could be repurposed for harm, will be crucial in anticipating and mitigating potential risks. Respecting individuals' autonomy through informed consent, particularly in cases where AI systems play a role in influencing decisions, will be of utmost importance, as individuals interact with AI systems in increasingly nuanced ways.

ChatGPT: A Leader in AI Development

Of all the Natural Language Processing platforms to rise in recent years, ChatGPT has emerged as a remarkable success story. Developed by OpenAI, ChatGPT is a transformative step forward in the world of AI-driven language models.

First and foremost, ChatGPT's success can be attributed to its groundbreaking innovation in the field of NLP. ChatGPT is built on the formidable foundation of GPT-3, and it has been trained on an extensive corpus of text, enabling it to understand and generate human-like text with unique fluency and coherence. It has the ability to engage in meaningful and contextually relevant conversations, making it an amazing tool for various applications, from customer support chatbots to content generation.

ChatGPT's success also stems from its adaptability and versatility. It can seamlessly suit itself to various domains and industries, giving anyone a solution for just about any task. Its versatility means it can generate content for marketing, answer technical queries, assist with language translation, and even offer emotional support through empathetic conversations. This adaptability makes ChatGPT a valuable asset for both businesses and individuals.

One of the key factors contributing to ChatGPT's success is how easily it's integrated. OpenAI has made it accessible through an API, allowing developers and organizations to effortlessly incorporate its capabilities into their applications and services. This accessibility has democratized the power of advanced NLP, allowing smaller companies and developers to use ChatGPT's capabilities, creating innovation and creativity in the NLP space.

ChatGPT's success also rests on its constant improvement and learning capabilities. OpenAI actively seeks user feedback and iterates upon the model to address its limitations and enhance its performance. This approach means consistent and real improvements, making ChatGPT more reliable, context-aware, and able to handle a wider array of tasks over time.

Another vital aspect of ChatGPT's success is its commitment to ethical and responsible AI. OpenAI has implemented measures to prevent the generation of harmful or biased content, showing that AI technologies can and do benefit society at large. This ethical stance has earned the trust of users and regulators.

ChatGPT's success extends beyond its technical prowess; it has also fostered a vibrant community of users and developers. This community-driven approach has led to many tools, libraries, and resources that enhance ChatGPT's capabilities and ease of use. There is a collaborative spirit surrounding ChatGPT, marking and contributing to its ongoing success.

ChatGPT's success as an NLP model is a testament to its groundbreaking innovation, adaptability, ease of integration, continuous improvement, ethical considerations, and the strong community it has formed around it. As it continues to evolve and push the boundaries of what is possible in NLP, ChatGPT is an example of the positive impact AI can have on all spheres of society.

Government Policies and Regulations

In tandem with ethical considerations and industry changes, the establishment of global governance and regulatory frameworks for AI development and deployment will be instrumental in shaping how AI technologies are adopted and integrated into various aspects of society. Upholding ethical standards in AI research and development will be fundamental in preventing the creation of systems that could inadvertently cause harm or perpetuate societal injustices. The coming years will witness ongoing collaboration between researchers, policymakers, industry leaders, and ethicists as they work together to navigate this intricate integration.

While significant progress has already been made in the development of AI policies, there is still plenty of room for improvement.

Several countries and regions have begun implementing policies and regulations related to artificial intelligence. These policies primarily focused on areas such as data privacy, transparency, accountability, and ethical use of AI technologies. For instance, the European Union introduced the General Data Protection Regulation which included provisions for the ethical use of AI and automated decision-making systems. Additionally, the EU proposed the Artificial Intelligence Act in 2021, which aims to regulate high-risk AI applications.

In the United States, there were no comprehensive federal AI regulations at that time, but various states introduced their own measures. Furthermore, organizations like the National Institute of Standards and Technology developed frameworks to guide the ethical development and use of AI. The private sector also played a role in setting ethical standards and best practices, with companies like Google and Microsoft issuing their own AI ethics guidelines.

Despite these efforts, there are still significant gaps in AI policy. Many existing regulations struggle to keep up with the rapid pace of technological advancement, and enforcement mechanisms are generally quite limited.

Additionally, the definition of what constitutes "high-risk" AI applications varies, leading to inconsistencies in regulatory approaches.

To improve current policies, several measures could be considered. Firstly, a more cohesive and standardized approach to AI regulation on a global scale would help address the transnational nature of AI technologies. This could involve international cooperation and the establishment of common frameworks. Secondly, there should be a focus on ongoing education and awareness programs to ensure that stakeholders, including developers, users, and policymakers, have a clear understanding of the ethical implications of AI. Thirdly, increased investment in research and development of AI technologies with an ethical and transparent focus is crucial to fostering innovation in a responsible manner.

Furthermore, it is essential to establish robust mechanisms for auditing and verifying compliance with AI regulations, possibly through the use of third-party certifications or regulatory bodies.

Finally, AI policies should be designed with flexibility in mind to adapt to rapidly evolving technologies and potentially unforeseen challenges.

How to Prepare for the Future of AI

As we step into the realm of Artificial Intelligence business utility, it's essential to approach it strategically. Begin by establishing a solid foundation in AI basics, understanding its potential applications, and how they align with your business objectives. This knowledge will serve as the compass guiding your journey toward more efficient and productive operations.

Next, pinpoint specific challenges or opportunities within your business that AI can address. This is akin to setting the destination on your roadmap, providing a clear direction for implementation. It's crucial to have a well-defined goal to work towards.

Equipping yourself with practical skills is akin to packing the right tools for the journey. Invest time in mastering data handling, preprocessing, and basic programming. These skills are the building blocks that empower you to work effectively with data, a pivotal aspect of training AI models and gaining meaningful insights.

Starting small with pilot projects is a practical way to test the waters. These projects serve as controlled environments to showcase the tangible value of AI within your business. Remember, it's not just about the results; it's also about building confidence and excitement among your team.

Leveraging pre-built tools and services from major cloud platforms like AWS, Google Cloud, and Azure can significantly expedite the integration of AI into your operations. These platforms offer user-friendly AI services that can be seamlessly integrated, even if you don't possess extensive technical expertise.

Ensuring data quality and privacy is akin to reinforcing the foundation of your AI initiatives. Make sure your data is clean, reliable, and complies with privacy regulations. This is paramount for training accurate and reliable AI models and gaining trust in the insights they provide.

Embrace an iterative approach of experimentation, measurement, and adaptation. Test different AI solutions, monitor their performance, and be ready to make adjustments based on the results. This ongoing process of refinement is what maximizes the impact of your AI initiatives.

Lastly, maintain a strong ethical stance and stay adaptable to new developments. Uphold ethical considerations in every AI initiative, ensuring responsible practices and respect for individual rights. Stay curious about emerging AI trends and technologies, as this will position you to seize new opportunities as they arise.

In summary, integrating AI into your business operations is an informative and transformative journey. Each step is a deliberate move towards more efficient and innovative practices.

What AI Thinks

ChatGPT: "The future of AI holds exciting possibilities with advancements in areas like natural language understanding, autonomous systems, and medical diagnostics. AI is expected to become more integrated into daily life, impacting industries from healthcare to transportation, while also raising challenges in ethics, privacy, and human-AI collaboration. Continued research, collaboration, and responsible development will shape AI's evolution, leading to innovative solutions and transformative changes in various aspects of society."

Conclusion

Welcome to the end of the beginning! Our journey into AI so far has taken us through numerous industries, revelations, and strategies but it is really just the beginning. Far more lies ahead and the possibilities for AI seem almost endless.

We've discussed its profound impact on healthcare, where it enhances diagnostics and patient interaction. Moreover, we've covered how AI is revolutionizing fields like finance, investing, real estate, marketing, online business, and content creation, pushing the boundaries of human imagination.

Stand-out features like NLP chatbots, predictive analytics, machine learning, and task automation are just the tip of the iceberg. The potential that we can squeeze from AI is up to us.

Admittedly, the integration of AI into every industry is not without challenges. The parallel problems of ethical considerations, data privacy, and transparency remain important concerns that will require thoughtful and continuous deliberation. But when approached with care and foresight, AI definitively emerges as a powerful ally, augmenting human capabilities and enabling us to tackle complex problems with unprecedented efficiency.

The Next Frontier

We stand on the precipice of a grand future, where AI promises to ignite our imagination and reshape the world as we know it. Picture a world where machines amplify our creativity, shedding light on unexplored realms and unraveling the complexities of our universe. Even what were once considered medical miracles may become routine, all thanks to AI's relentless pursuit of knowledge.

Beyond the confines of the present, AI offers us a tantalizing glimpse into a realm where the boundaries of art, music, and expression blur, giving birth to symphonies and masterpieces that transcend human limitations. It empowers us to dream bigger, to delve deeper, and to dare venture where imagination knows no bounds.

Yet, this journey is far from solitary; it is a collective endeavor. Together, we will forge pathways of understanding, sculpting a future where AI empowers us all. The collaborative dance between minds, disciplines, and cultures will propel us forward, uncovering new realms of possibility.

What lies ahead is just the beginning. Even greater AI tools and innovations are on the horizon, waiting to amplify our capabilities and lead us into uncharted territories of knowledge and creativity. Every step forward will be fueled by the boundless potential of human-AI collaboration.

One might even be forgiven for asking: Can we keep up and manage to stay in the saddle as AI and business race onward?

The Influence Of Artificial General Intelligence On Humanity

Artificial General Intelligence (AGI) is the next evolutionary step for AI. This promises a level of cognitive capability that may surpass even human intelligence, raising both profound opportunities and profound questions.

What is AGI? How can it help us reach new heights of autonomy and efficacy? How can we ensure its ethical deployment and what responsibilities will accompany this new beast?

Imagine a digital mind capable of not only mastering complex tasks but also learning and adapting across a multitude of domains, mirroring the expansive cognitive abilities of the human brain. It is both awe-inspiring and terrifying.

A simple comparison is this:

AI is a really smart tool, like a super advanced calculator. It can perform specific tasks really well, like solving math problems, writing a social media post, or helping you find patterns in your data.

AGI is a genius all-rounder, like a super intelligent person. This person not only solves math problems but can also paint, cook, write novels, and even learn new things they've never encountered before. They're versatile and can adapt to many different tasks, just like AGI can adapt to various types of tasks without needing to be specifically programmed for each one.

Delving into these intriguing questions requires embarking on a brand new journey to understand the implications and potential of AGI.

Know this: our future is tightly woven with technology. Artificial Intelligence now stands at the forefront, versatile and full of potential. It touches every aspect of our lives, from self-driving cars in busy streets to deciphering complex medical data. It's a pivotal part of our progress toward a better and brighter world.

However, with these advancements, we must remember to proceed with care and wisdom. Let empathy guide our actions, and let ethics be our compass.

In every adventure with AI, we have the power to shape a brighter future. It's a canvas where we build on the dreams of generations. So, let's move forward with curiosity and purpose. In this new world, we hold the power to create a legacy that will echo through time.

AI is unleashed. It is dynamic, diverse, and full of possibility. Whether you work in finance or fiction, join the AI revolution and boost your business and creativity now!

What AI Thinks about AGI

ChatGPT: "Artificial General Intelligence (AGI) refers to a level of artificial intelligence where machines possess human-like cognitive abilities, enabling them to understand, learn, and perform any intellectual task that a human can do. AGI would have the capacity to excel in various domains without being limited to specific tasks, showcasing a broad range of general intelligence capabilities. Achieving AGI is a complex challenge that involves creating machines with consciousness, adaptability, and the ability to reason across diverse contexts."

References

Boucher, T. (2023, May 15). *"I'm making thousands using AI to write books."* Newsweek. https://www.newsweek.com/ai-books-art-money-artificial-intelligence-1799923

Dartmouth. (n.d.). *Artificial Intelligence (AI) Coined at Dartmouth | Dartmouth.* Home.dartmouth.edu. https://home.dartmouth.edu/about/artificial-intelligence-ai-coined-dartmouth

Fjeld, J., Achten, N., Hilligoss, H., Nagy, A., & Srikumar, M. (2020). Principled Artificial Intelligence: Mapping Consensus in Ethical and Rights-Based Approaches to Principles for AI. *SSRN Electronic Journal.* https://doi.org/10.2139/ssrn.3518482

Luo, Q., Bu, J., Xu, W., & Huang, D. (2023). Stock market volatility prediction: Evidence from a new bagging model. *International Review of Economics & Finance, 87,* 445–456. https://doi.org/10.1016/j.iref.2023.05.008

Moore, G.E. (1998). *Cramming More Components Onto Integrated Circuits.* Proceedings of the IEEE, 86, 82-85.

Precedence Research. (n.d.). *Generative AI In Real Estate Market Size, Report 2023-2032.* Www.precedenceresearch.com. Retrieved September 14, 2023, from https://www.precedenceresearch.com/generative-ai-in-real-estate-market

Urban Land Institute. (2023). *EMERGING TRENDS IN REAL ESTATE* ®. https://www.pwc.com/us/en/industries/financial-services/images/pwc-emerging-trends-in-real-estate-2023.pdf

Wallach, W. (2009). *Moral machines : teaching robots right from wrong.* In *Internet Archive.* Oxford : Oxford University Press. https://archive.org/details/moralmachinestea0000wall/page/n 9/mode/2up

Zliobaite, Indre. (2017). *Fairness-aware machine learning: a perspective.*

Unlock the World of AI Terminology!

Congratulations on completing your journey through the fascinating world of Artificial Intelligence in seven industries. We hope this book has provided you with valuable insights and knowledge about the incredible possibilities that AI offers.

To further aid you in your exploration of AI, we're excited to offer you a **FREE AI Terminology Guide.** This comprehensive glossary includes definitions for a wide range of AI-related terms, helping you navigate the often complex and evolving landscape of artificial intelligence with ease.

In this AI Terminology Guide, you'll find concise explanations for key concepts, algorithms, and technologies, ensuring that you have a handy reference at your fingertips whenever you encounter technical jargon in the world of AI.

To claim your free AI Terminology Guide, simply scan the QR code and enter your email address.

We'll send you a downloadable PDF copy right away, so you can have it ready whenever you need to refresh your memory or deepen your understanding of AI terminology.

Thank you for joining us on this AI adventure, and we look forward to continuing to support your AI exploration in the future. Stay curious, keep learning, and embrace the exciting world of Artificial Intelligence!

"Artificial intelligence is a tool, not a threat." Rodney Brooks

Warm regards,

Derek Wells

Made in United States
Troutdale, OR
12/08/2024

26052015R00080